$492

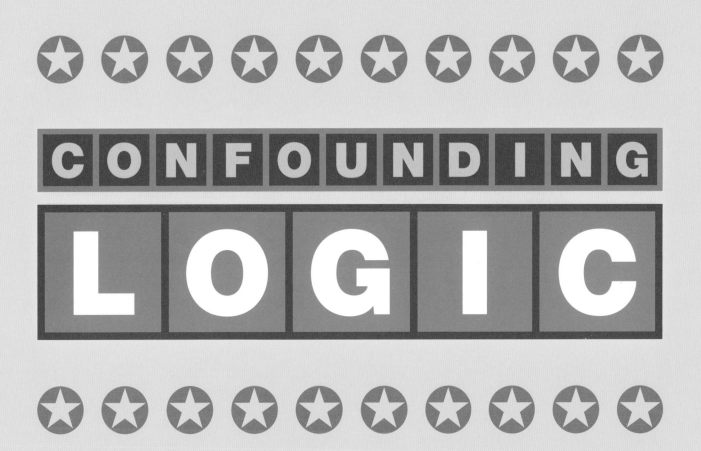

CONFOUNDING LOGIC

THUNDER BAY
P·R·E·S·S

San Diego, California

Thunder Bay Press
An imprint of the Advantage Publishers Group
5880 Oberlin Drive, San Diego, CA 92121-4794
www.thunderbaybooks.com

All notations of errors or omissions should be addressed to Thunder Bay Press, Editorial Department, at the above address. All other correspondence (author inquiries, permissions) concerning the content of this book should be addressed to Book Creation Ltd., 20 Lochaline Street, London W6 9SH, United Kingdom; E-mail: info@librios.com

ISBN 1-59223-354-6

Printed and bound in China
1 2 3 4 5   09 08 07 06 05

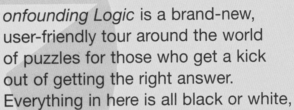

Confounding Logic is a brand-new, user-friendly tour around the world of puzzles for those who get a kick out of getting the right answer. Everything in here is all black or white, right or wrong, so there'll be no arguments—apart from whose turn it is to try the next puzzle!

Logic plays a vital part of the modern world. By using high and low voltages, computers can represent decisions such as TRUE and FALSE or store the binary digits 0 and 1. Putting many of these basic elements together allows for more complex computer programs and the ability to store data sequences. Without this Boolean logic, named after the mathematician George Boole, modern industry and commerce could not function. Furthermore, the whole of mathematics in general can be boiled down to a series of very logical statements. This astounding result was proved by the famous mathematicians Bertrand Russell and Alfred North Whitehead in the 1910s. Russell was later quoted as saying, "My intellect never quite recovered from the strain!"

Computers are now so good at logic that humans are now trying to make them act less logically, so that they mirror the behavior of humans. Programmers call this "fuzzy logic," where a computer's thought processes can range between all values from 0 (false) to 1 (true), rather than just the two extremes. This allows computers to think in terms of what "probably" or "might just" happen, and plan strategically accordingly. Advanced AI (artifical intelligence) programs using fuzzy logic are written in many of today's popular computer games.

Nuances of logic can be surprisingly subtle. For example, suppose we asked you to describe whether the statement "Some birds have black feathers" is always, sometimes, or never true. Many people are tempted to choose "sometimes" because the statement appears conditional. However, the correct answer is "always" because there are always some birds somewhere in the world that have black feathers. What if we asked you to describe the truth of the statement "Some birds are ugly"? In this instance, none of the three answers can be chosen because the statement is a matter of opinion and there's no right or wrong answer. These distinctions, subtle though they are, form the basis for some branches of philosophy.

So if you're dying to test out your own powers of deduction, where to head next? You could go straight through the book tackling each one as it comes. However, if you want to ease yourself in more gently, look for our special grading system. Each puzzle is rated from 1 to 10 stars. Low numbers of stars indicate that the puzzle shouldn't deter you too long. An 8-, 9- or 10-star problem means you're likely to be taxed to your limit. Furthermore, there are time limits to keep an eye on, just to increase the tension that little bit more.

By the end of this book, you'll be a master of deducing right from wrong. And that's the truth. ✲

—David Bodycombe

1 DIFFICULTY ✪✪✪✪✪☆☆☆☆☆  **5** Minutes

If you think tic-tac-toe is boring, try this interesting variation. The aim of the game is to avoid winning—in other words, if you get three of your symbol in a horizontal, vertical, or diagonal line, you lose the game.

In the sample game shown, it is O's turn. Can you see which of the four possibilities (A, B, C, or D) will lead to a guaranteed win?

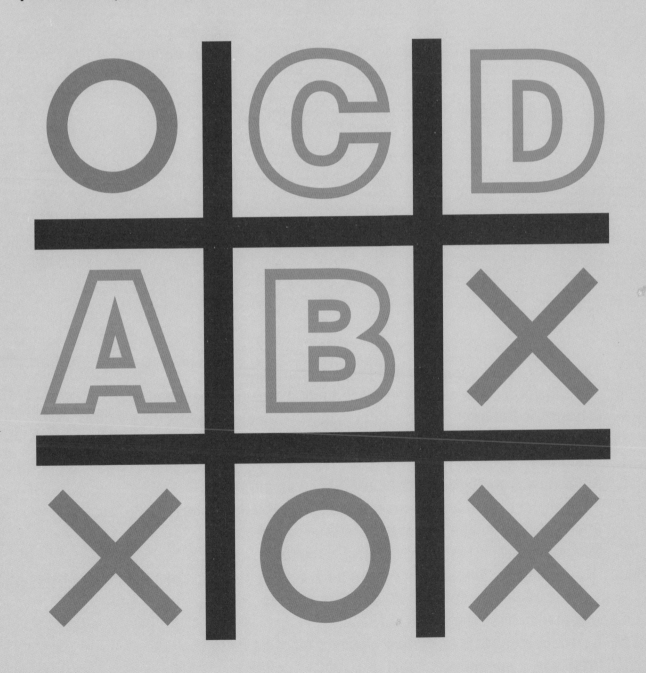

2 DIFFICULTY ✪✪✪✪✪✪✪✪✪✪

7 Minutes

Can you crack the safe? First decide which of the 14 statements given are false, then shade out the areas on the combination lock that are labeled with the letters of those false statements (so if you think statement A is false, shade out area A). The remaining lit segments will give you the digital combination required.

Hint: three of the statements are false.

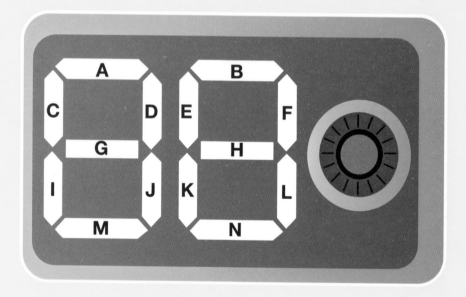

A. The upper number in a fraction is the numerator.
B. The ratio of a circle's circumference to its diameter is called pi.
C. A league is the term for a nautical mile.
D. Euclid wrote a famous work on geometry.
E. The Roman numeral for 500 is D.
F. An irrational number cannot be expressed as a fraction.
G. The longest side of a right-angled triangle is the hypotenuse.
H. Andrew Wiles famously proved Fermat's last theorem.
I. Integral and differential are types of calculus.
J. Hexadecimal is the number system for counting in groups of 12.
K. A reflex angle has between 90 and 180 degrees.
L. A heptagon has seven sides.
M. A perfect number is equal to the sum of all of its factors.
N. Originally, a myriad was equal to 10,000.

3 DIFFICULTY ✪✪✪✪✪✪✪✪✪✪  3 Minutes

Each block is equal to the sum of the two numbers beneath it.
Can you find all the missing numbers?

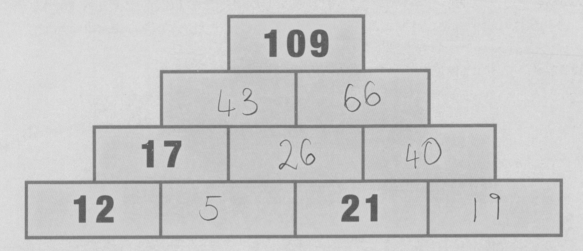

4 DIFFICULTY ✪✪✪✪✪✪✪✪✪✪ 6 Minutes

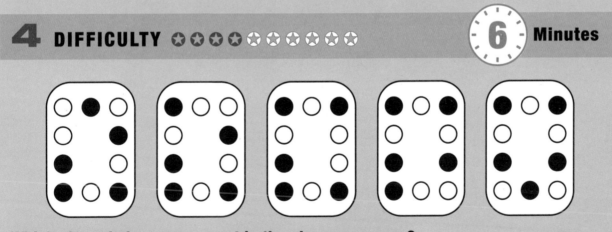

Which shape below comes next in the above sequence?

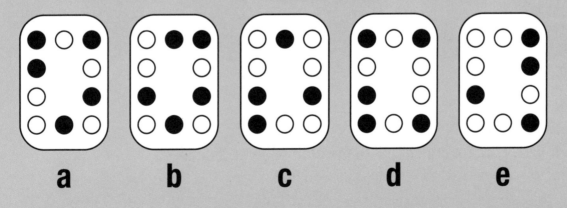

a   b   c   d   e

5 DIFFICULTY ✪✪✪✪✪✪✪✪✪✪ **6** Minutes

Can you fit these numbers into the grid? One number has already been inserted to help you get started.

3 DIGITS	5 DIGITS	7 DIGITS
135	18915	1767463
208	21266	2096913
424	24437	2678374
650	32791	3235488
	43420	4937541
4 DIGITS	55159	4965907
1543	61605	5244243
2246	79937	5997845
4225	82314	6583226
5890	90556	6796588
6134		7216860
7979	**6 DIGITS**	8822997
8199	~~130471~~	9124965
9484	530395	9721305
	766860	
	897030	

6 DIFFICULTY

 Minutes

Each row and column contains the same numbers and signs, but they are arranged in a different order each time. Find the correct order to arrive at the final totals shown.

2	+	6	x	3	–	4	=	20
							=	10
							=	16
							=	17
=		=		=		=		
8		13		2		24		

7 DIFFICULTY ⊛⊛⊛⊛⊛☆☆☆☆☆

5 Minutes

Make a calculation totaling the figure on the right by inserting the four mathematical operators (+, −, ÷, x) between the numbers shown.

They can be inserted in any order, and one of them has been used twice.

| 2 | | 3 | | 8 | | 7 | | 5 | | 4 | = | 6 |

8 DIFFICULTY ⊛⊛⊛⊛⊛☆☆☆☆☆

8 Minutes

Five hopefuls brought their animals to the county fair. Can you figure out whose animal won which prize, and what kind of animal it was?

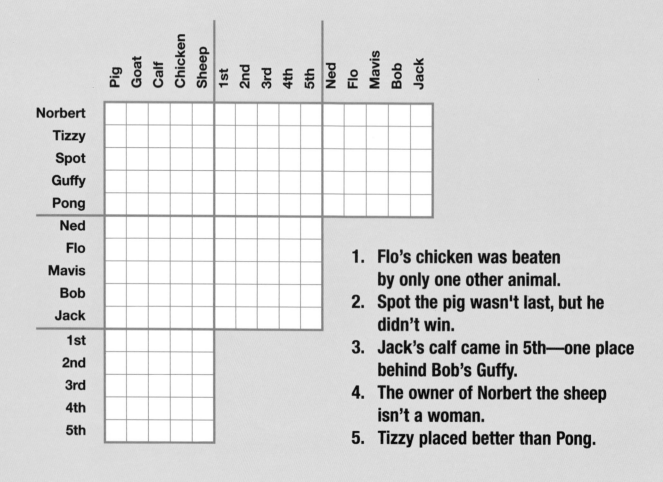

1. Flo's chicken was beaten by only one other animal.
2. Spot the pig wasn't last, but he didn't win.
3. Jack's calf came in 5th—one place behind Bob's Guffy.
4. The owner of Norbert the sheep isn't a woman.
5. Tizzy placed better than Pong.

9 DIFFICULTY ✪✪✪✪✪✪✪✪✪✪  Minute

Study these shapes for one minute, then see if you can answer the questions on page 14.

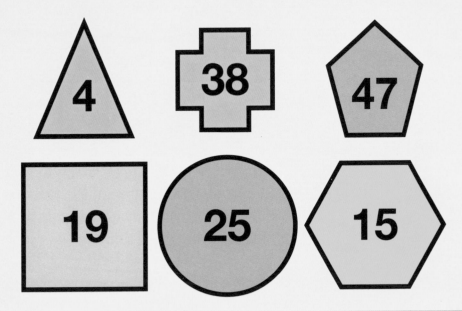

10 DIFFICULTY ✪✪✪✪✪✪✪✪✪✪  Minutes

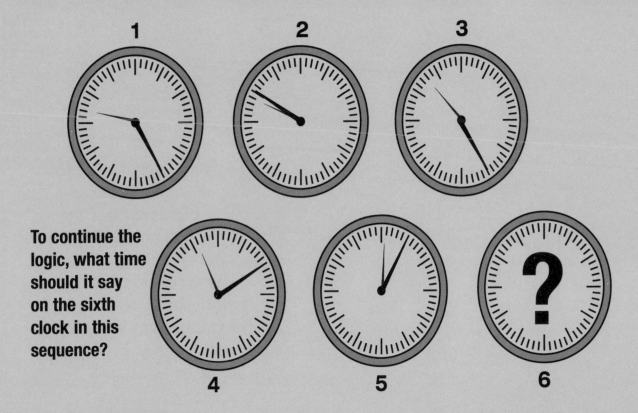

To continue the logic, what time should it say on the sixth clock in this sequence?

[9] DIFFICULTY ✪✪✪✪✪✪✪✪✪✪  **3** Minutes

Can you answer these questions about the puzzle on page 13 without looking back?

1. How many shapes have odd numbers?
2. Which three numbers will total a fourth number shown?
3. What is the total when you multiply the number on the blue shape by that on the shape directly above the blue shape?
4. Which shapes have even numbers?
5. What is the total of the numbers on the green shapes?
6. What is the total when you add the number on the pink shape to that on the circle, then subtract this total from the number on the pentagon?
7. Which two shapes of the same color are horizontally next to one another?
8. What is the total of the three numbers in the shapes on the top row?

11 DIFFICULTY ✪✪✪✪✪✪✪✪✪✪ **7** Minutes

There is a hidden phrase in the grid of letters. Place the right-hand grid over the letter grid in three different ways and then reassemble the resulting letters to see what you have "won."

12 DIFFICULTY ✪✪✪✪✪✪✪✪✪✪ 30 Minutes

You'll be flying high if you solve this numeropic. Use the rules below to help you understand how to complete this puzzle.

How to do a numeropic:

Along each row or column, there are numbers that indicate how many blocks of black squares are in a line. For example, "3, 4, 5" indicates that from left to right or top to bottom, there is a group of three black squares, then a group of four black squares, then another group of five black squares.

Each block of black squares on the same line must have at least one white square between it and the next block of black squares. Blocks of black squares may or may not have a number of white squares before and after them.

It is sometimes possible to determine which squares will be black without reference to other lines or columns. It is helpful to put a small dot in a square you know will be empty.

				7	6	6	4											2				2							
	8	8	8	3	4	4	2	4		4		3		2		1		4			7	2	2	1	1				
	1	1	2	5	4	3	2	2	4	1	4	4	2	4	1	4	1	3	9	8	1	5	3	3	4	4	6	7	8
8	2	3	4	1	1	2	3	1	2	4	8	3	8	3	8	3	8	5	6	6	5	1	4	4	3	3	2	2	1
1	2	5	7	7	7	7	7	11	11	6	2	2	2	3	3	4	5	1	1	1	1	1	1	2	2	2	3	4	5
2	1	1	1	1	1	1	1	1	2	2	2	2	3	4	5	5	6	5	6	5	6	5	6	5	4	3	3	2	3

			5	1
			7	2
			9	10
		12	6	1
		13	3	2
		16	4	3
	7	6	5	5
		4	5	6
		2	6	7
	7	4	1	8
	10	7	3	3
		3	4	2
				8
	9	4	3	11
		7	8	11
	5	4	3	10
	3	8	9	1
1	4	3	8	3
		8	7	4
	1	4	5	6
	4	3	4	2
			10	1
		10	1	1
		9	1	1
9	1	1	1	1
			8	10
			6	12
		4	15	1
			1	21
				30

13 DIFFICULTY ✪✪✪✪✪✪✩✩✩  **4** Minutes

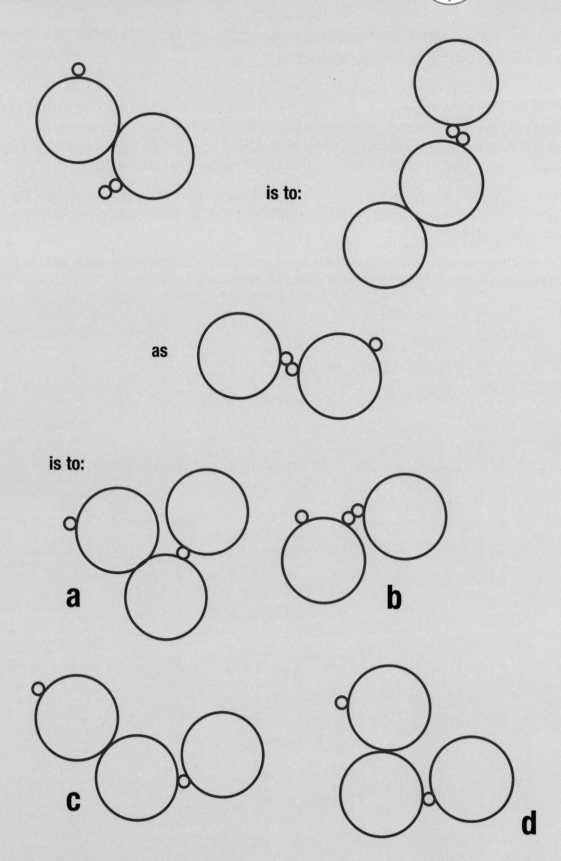

is to:

as

is to:

a

b

c

d

14 DIFFICULTY ✪✪✪✪✪✪✪✪✪✪  2 Minutes

In what way are the start and end of each of these six times identical?

9:57	8:23
1:32	11:25
9:13	2:48

15 DIFFICULTY ✪✪✪✪✪✪✪✪✪✪  5 Minutes

Place the remaining pieces in the grid so that:
* each row and column has two red and two yellow squares, and
* no row or column has two of the same digit.

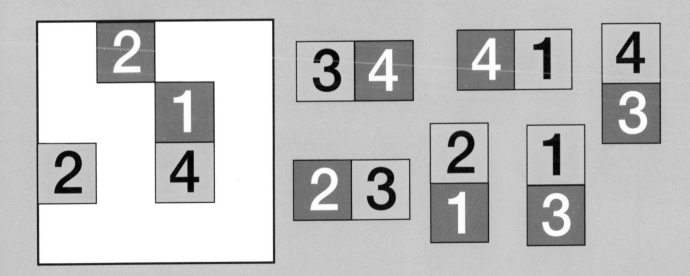

16 DIFFICULTY ✪✪✪✩✩✩✩✩✩✩  **3** Minutes

Which of the four boxed figures (a, b, c, or d) completes the set?

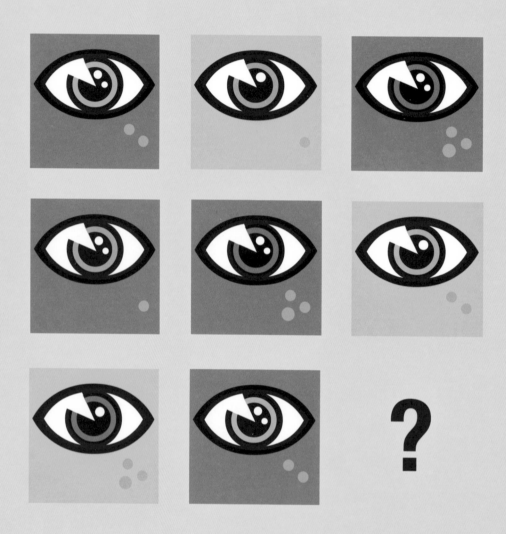

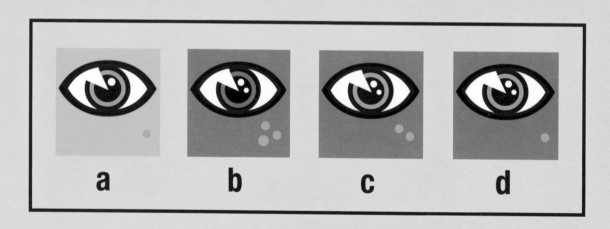

a b c d

17 DIFFICULTY ✪✪✪✪✪✪✪✪✪✪

8 Minutes

Try to get from the top left red square to the bottom right red square by making a series of calculations. You must always move from each square to an adjacent one and may not move diagonally.

8	÷	0	=	8	÷	2
−	1	=	9	÷	1	=
9	+	3	=	3	x	4
=	0	x	6	−	7	+
6	=	2	=	8	=	3
÷	2	=	4	=	8	−
1	=	3	x	9	+	3
=	3	x	2	÷	0	=
6	÷	3	=	2	=	8

18 DIFFICULTY ✪✪✪✪☆☆☆☆☆☆

3 Minutes

The number 123987 appears just once in this grid and occurs in a straight line, running either backward or forward in a horizontal, vertical, or diagonal direction. Can you locate it?

9	3	2	1	7	3	1	2	3	8	9	7
7	8	2	2	8	9	1	2	3	9	8	2
1	3	1	7	3	2	2	2	2	9	3	1
9	2	2	8	3	1	3	9	1	8	2	2
7	8	3	1	2	3	7	7	7	3	1	3
8	7	9	3	2	1	8	8	9	2	8	9
3	1	7	7	9	3	9	1	1	7	8	7
2	2	8	9	3	3	7	2	2	3	2	8
1	2	3	9	2	2	3	8	3	2	7	7
7	1	8	1	3	9	1	1	9	1	8	3
8	3	1	2	3	7	9	8	7	3	9	2
9	7	1	2	3	8	7	9	3	2	1	1

19 DIFFICULTY ✪✪✪✪✪☆☆☆☆☆ | ⏱ **5** Minutes

Each block is equal to the sum of the two numbers beneath it. Can you find all the missing numbers?

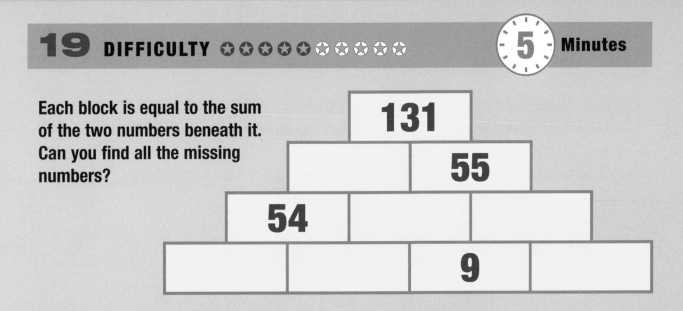

20 DIFFICULTY ✪☆☆☆☆☆☆☆☆☆ | ⏱ **10** Minutes

Take the cards to the left of the grid and place them so that each horizontal row and vertical column contains a joker plus four aces of different suits, and each shape (shown by the thick lines) also contains a joker plus four aces of different suits. Some cards are already in place.

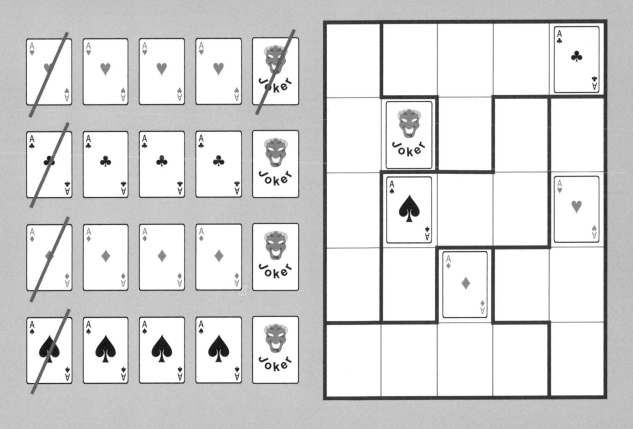

21 DIFFICULTY ✪✪✪✪✪✪✪✪✪✪  **3** Minutes

Make a calculation totaling the figure on the right by inserting the four mathematical operators (+, −, ÷, x) between the numbers shown.

They can be inserted in any order, and one of them has been used twice.

| 9 | 3 | 6 | 2 | 4 | 5 | = | 10 |

22 DIFFICULTY ✪✪✪✪✪✪✪✪✪✪  **5** Minutes

Given that scales a and b balance perfectly, how many circles are needed to balance scale c?

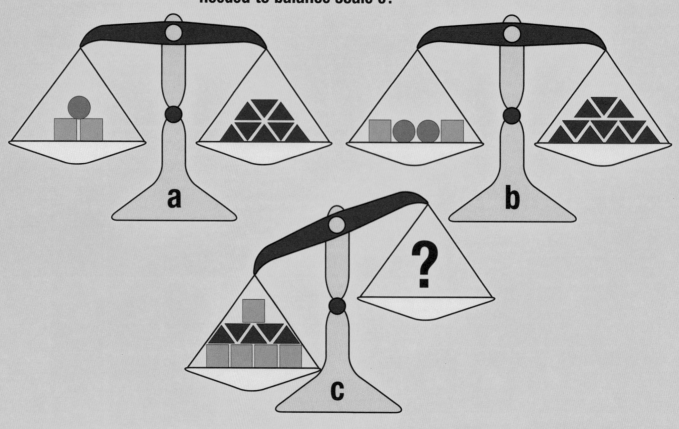

23 **DIFFICULTY** ✪✪✪✪✩✩✩✩ **3** **Minutes**

Which of these configurations is the odd one out?

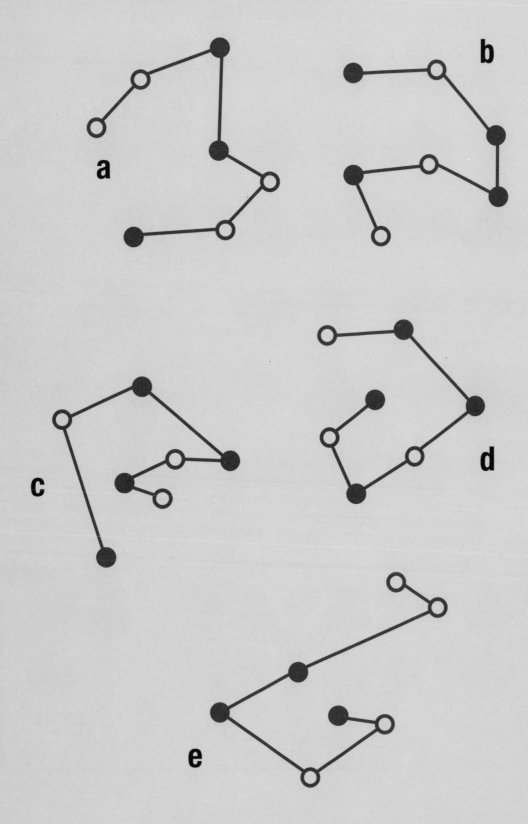

 **6** Minutes

Which of the four boxed figures (a, b, c, or d) completes the set?

a   b   c   d

25 DIFFICULTY ✪✪✪✪✪✪✪✪✪✪

5 Minutes

Can you fit these numbers into the grid? One number has already been inserted to help you get started.

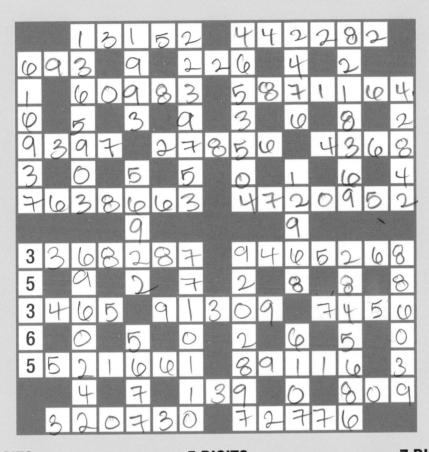

3 DIGITS
- 199
- 226
- 693
- 809

4 DIGITS
- 1993
- 2476
- 3465
- 4368
- 5677
- 6107
- 7456
- 9397

5 DIGITS
- 12968
- 13152
- 27836
- 35365
- 42842
- 56922
- 60983
- 72776
- 89116
- 91309

6 DIGITS
- 320730
- 442282
- 616937
- 836039

7 DIGITS
- 1365903
- 2239753
- 2845686
- 3368287
- 4653504
- 4720952
- 5521661
- 5871164
- 6960242
- 7638663
- 7710110
- 8218369
- 9202897 ✓
- 9465268

26 DIFFICULTY ✪✪✪✪✪✪☆☆☆☆

8 Minutes

Five models each wore one of five items by five designers on the catwalk. Can you figure out each model's last name and which item, by which designer, each wore?

1. Ms. Jones didn't wear Vergucci, carry a bag, or wear gloves or blue.
2. The pink hat wasn't Fundi or Tom Buick, and Kate didn't wear it.
3. Naomi Taylor didn't wear gloves or shoes.
4. The Vergucci bag wasn't red.
5. Manon works for Armande, which doesn't make hats or gloves.
6. Jody wore all black but not Canale, and she didn't wear a coat.
7. Miss Dupris wore gold but not by Fundi or Armande, and she didn't wear gloves.
8. Ms. Briant wore Canale.
9. Tom Buick's collection was all blue.

	Jones	Dupris	Heaton	Taylor	Briant	Tom Buick	Vergucci	Canale	Fundi	Armande	Gloves	Hat	Bag	Shoes	Coat	Red	Blue	Pink	Gold	Black
Jody																				
Kate																				
Naomi																				
Emma																				
Manon																				
Red																				
Blue																				
Pink																				
Gold																				
Black																				
Gloves																				
Hat																				
Bag																				
Shoes																				
Coat																				
Tom Buick																				
Vergucci																				
Canale																				
Fundi																				
Armande																				

27 DIFFICULTY ✪✪✪✪✪☆☆☆☆☆

5 Minutes

Which pentagon from the selection below should replace the question mark?

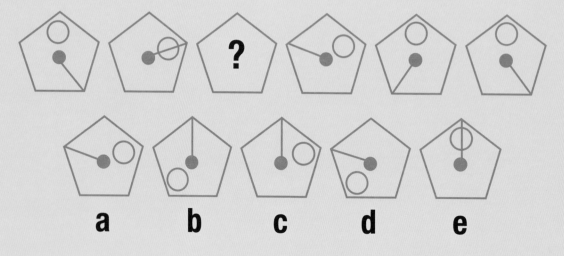

a   **b**   **c**   **d**   **e**

28 DIFFICULTY ✪✪✪✪✪✩✩✩✩✩

Here's a very simple but effective game. Take 15 coins (it doesn't matter how they are arranged). Two players take turns picking up one, two, or three coins. Play continues until there are no coins left in the pile. The winner is the person who ends up with an odd number of coins.

Play the game a few times and see if you can figure out a winning strategy. The player who goes first always has the advantage, if he or she knows how to use it properly! For a variation, try starting with 13 coins.

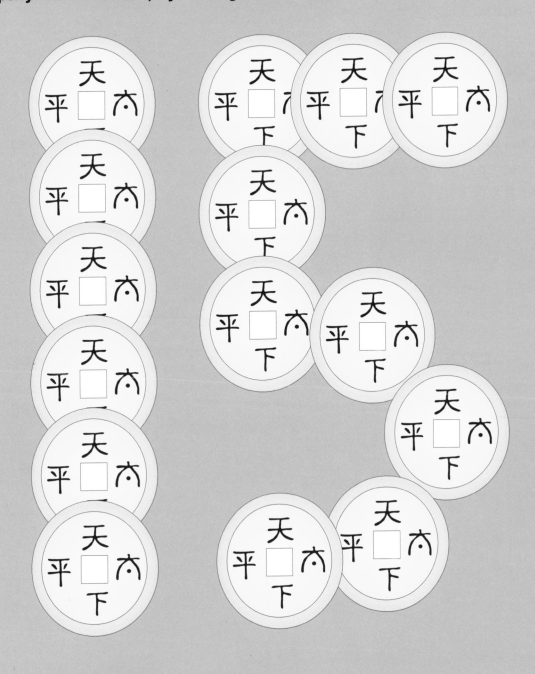

29 DIFFICULTY ✪✪✪✪✪✩✩✩✩✩  **5** Minutes

Given that scales a and b balance perfectly, how many gooseberries are needed to balance scale c?

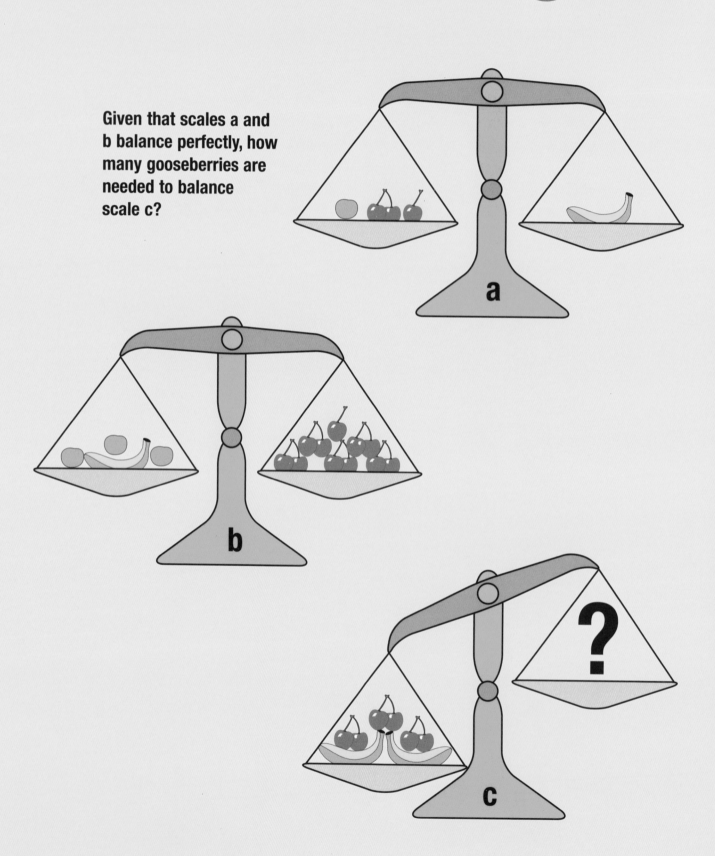

30 DIFFICULTY ✪✪✪✪✪✪✪✪✪✪  **3** Minutes

What number comes next?

49, 62, 70, 77, 91, 101, 103, ?

31 DIFFICULTY ✪✪✪✪✪✪✪✪✪✪  **4** Minutes

Which number is the odd one out?

7141 9187
3025 6140
8164 5149
2079 4193

32 DIFFICULTY ★★★☆☆☆☆☆☆☆  **4** Minutes

Each row and column contains the same numbers and signs, but they are arranged in a different order each time. Find the correct order to arrive at the final totals shown.

5	+	4	x	2	−	7	=	11
							=	13
							=	4
							=	25
=		=		=		=		
16		6		7		17		

33 DIFFICULTY ✪✪✪✪✪✪✩✩✩✩

 **Minutes**

The number 246135 appears just once in this grid and occurs in a straight line, running either backward or forward in a horizontal, vertical, or diagonal direction. Can you locate it?

2	4	6	2	4	6	1	6	4	2	5	4
4	4	3	5	6	5	3	5	6	3	3	5
6	5	6	6	4	2	3	2	1	5	1	1
1	3	3	1	2	5	4	3	2	3	5	3
3	1	4	2	4	6	3	1	5	6	3	6
2	6	2	6	4	2	6	4	2	5	6	4
3	4	4	1	2	4	5	1	1	6	4	2
1	2	6	4	4	1	3	6	2	4	2	4
6	4	5	2	6	3	4	4	5	2	3	6
4	6	1	4	1	2	2	2	6	4	2	1
2	3	2	6	2	3	1	6	4	2	4	2
5	6	1	2	4	6	1	3	2	5	2	5

34 DIFFICULTY ✪✪✪✪✪✪✪✪✪✪  **4** Minutes

Make a calculation totaling the figure below by inserting the four mathematical operators (+, −, ÷, x) between the numbers shown.

They can be inserted in any order, and one of them has been used twice.

| 8 | | 4 | | 3 | | 5 | | 2 | | 6 | = | 3 |

35 DIFFICULTY ✪✪✪✪✪✪✪✪✪✪  **6** Minutes

Here's a trickier one! Using the same principle as above try to complete the calculation. One of the mathematical operators has been used twice.

| 99 | | 25 | | 36 | | 11 | | 22 | | 72 | = | 127 |

36 DIFFICULTY ✪✪✪✪✪✪✩✩✩✩

5 Minutes

Given that scales a and b balance perfectly, how many red balls are needed to balance scale c?

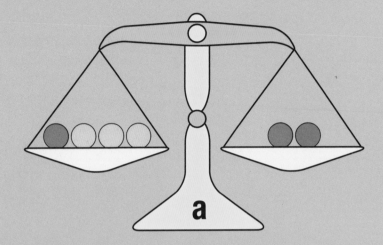

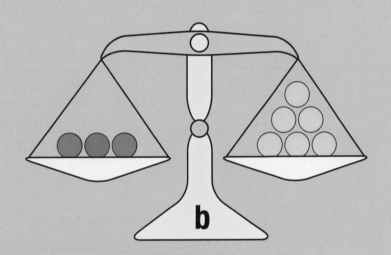

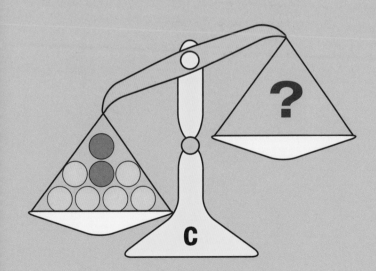

37 DIFFICULTY ★★★☆☆☆☆☆☆☆

3 Minutes

The number 619362 appears just once in this grid and occurs in a straight line, running either backward or forward in a horizontal, vertical, or diagonal direction. Can you locate it?

1	3	9	1	4	2	6	4	9	1	2	4
2	2	6	3	6	9	3	2	6	4	6	3
6	4	6	9	2	1	2	1	9	3	6	2
3	6	2	4	3	6	9	3	1	2	9	6
9	2	9	1	9	3	4	4	9	6	3	3
1	2	1	6	6	1	3	2	6	3	6	6
2	9	6	3	1	9	6	3	9	2	2	1
6	1	2	3	6	4	9	6	1	3	1	9
3	9	3	1	9	3	6	2	2	6	6	6
9	4	2	9	2	1	3	1	9	2	1	2
1	2	1	3	1	3	6	4	3	1	4	1
4	6	9	1	3	2	6	3	1	9	6	9

Place the remaining pieces in the grid so that:
* each row and column has two red and two yellow squares, and
* no row or column has two of the same digit.

2 **4**

4 **3**   **5** **2**

2

1   **4**   **5**

4   **1**   **3**

3

5 **1**

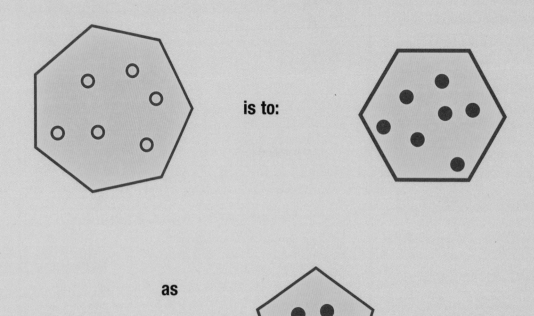

is to:

as

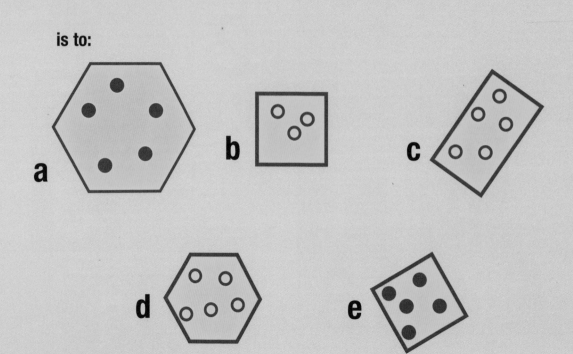

is to:

40 DIFFICULTY ★★★★★★★★★★  30 Minutes

See if you can rise to the challenge and complete this numeropic. See the panel on page 15 for instructions on how to complete this type of puzzle.

Column clues (top):

											2						
								1		1			2	1			
						1		2		6	1		8	2		1	
2	4	5	6	8		10	9		2	7	8	5	6		6	5	1	6	3	5
1	1	1	2	4	3	10	11	12	4	6	1	1	6	6	8	6	9	7	7	6	3	7	1	13		9	6	5	1
2	2	4	2	4	2	4	3	3	1	1	7	11	2	6	1	10	7	1	1	5	1	4	6	6	11	7	6	3	1
1	1	1	7	1	1	1	1	2	1	1	13	1	1	2	1	1	12	1	1	2	1	1	1	1	10	1	1	1	1

Row clues (left):

- 8
- 3 3
- 4 3
- 3 1 5 2
- 4 7 2
- 5 5 3
- 6 5 5
- 6 7 6
- 8 1 1 1 1 6
- 8 7
- 7 8 5
- 7 9 4
- 7 10 3
- 6 10 3
- 6 10 2
- 5 2 3 3 2
- 1 1 4 2 1 1 1 2 2
- 1 1 2 2 3 3 1 1
- 1 1 1 13 1
- 5 13 1
- 19 2
- 17 5
- 14 6
- 3 4 4 7
- 5 2 2 9
- 5 2 2 7
- 3 4 3 5
- 1 1 1 1 1 1 1 1
- 1 1 1 1 1 1 1
- 30

41 DIFFICULTY ✪✪✪✪✪☆☆☆☆☆  **5** Minutes

Each block is equal to the sum of the two numbers beneath it. Can you find all the missing numbers?

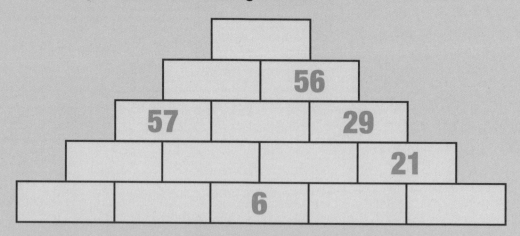

42 DIFFICULTY ✪✪✪✪☆☆☆☆☆☆  **3** Minutes

Where should the hour hand point to on clock e?

43 DIFFICULTY ✪✪✪✪✪✩✩✩✩  **12** **Minutes**

The ace, 2, 3, and 4 in each of four suits should be placed in the grid below. Digits and letters showing the values A, 2, 3, and 4 and the suits have been shown at the beginning of each row across and column down to indicate which values and suits are contained in those rows and columns. Can you figure out the unique place for each card?

44 DIFFICULTY ✪✪✪✪✪✪✪☆☆☆

 **30** Minutes

You'll probably be over the moon when you've completed this numeropic. See the panel on page 15 for instructions on how to complete this type of puzzle.

Column clues (top):

										1								2			
			4		4			4										3			
			1	4	2		6	3	7		11			2	2		3	3	4		
	2		4	1	1	1	4	5	5	2	1	1	8	5	10	1	11	11	6	4	2	3	5	7	16
	13	3	4	4	2	1	1	1	2	1	2	2	1	1	2	3	1	1	2	2	1	1	2	1	4	4	4	23
	6	18	10	8	8	8	1	6	1	1	1	1	1	1	3	2	1	1	3	3	4	6	6	1	7	2	2	2
30	30	5	4	3	3	4	5	14	1	7	6	5	4	3	2	1	6	6	4	2	1	3	3	7	2	1	4	4	3

Row clues (left):

				30
			14	15
		2	19	4
		3	19	3
		4	13	2
	4	4	6	2
	4	2	9	2
4	1	1	8	2
4 1 1	1	6	3	
4	2	1	4	4
	4	2	11	
	5	2	6	
	5	3	5	
6	4	2	4	
7	1	1	3	
8	1	1	2	
2 6	2	3	1	
10	2	4	1	
9 1	1	1	6	
9 1 1	1	1	4	
9 1	2	3	3	
4	3	1	5	2
3 3 1	3	3	1	
2	3	1	5	3
2	4	5	5	2
3 6 3 2	2	2	1	
4	8	4	2	5
	15	3	4	4
9	6	4	4	3
	22	4	2	

45 DIFFICULTY ✪✪✪✪✪✪✪✪✪✪ (**3**) **Minutes**

The number 302949 appears just once in this grid and occurs in a straight line, running either backward or forward in a horizontal, vertical, or diagonal direction. Can you locate it?

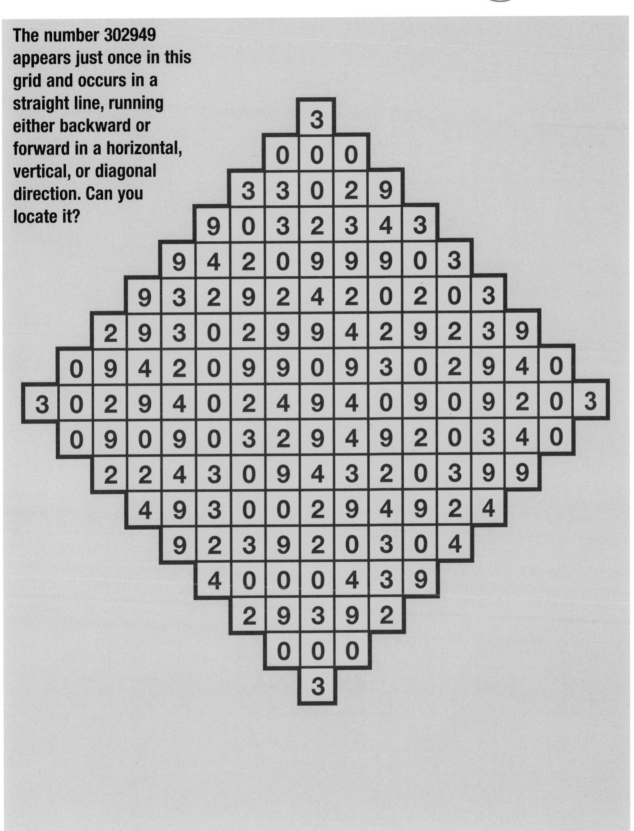

46 DIFFICULTY ✪✪✪✪✪✪✪✪✪✪   4 Minutes

What comes next in the above sequence?

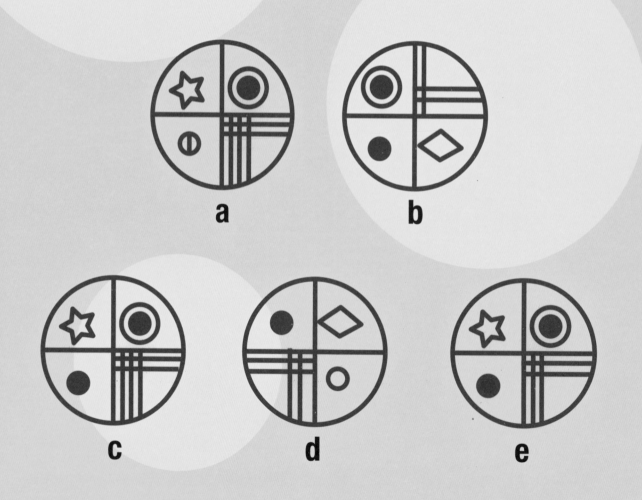

a   b

c   d   e

47 DIFFICULTY ✪✪✪✪✪✪✪✪✪✪ ⟨**2**⟩ Minutes

Which is the odd one out?

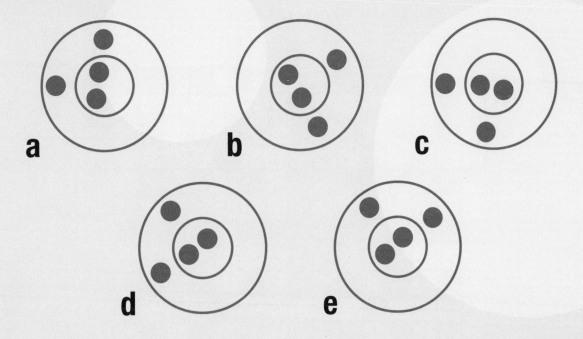

a   b   c

d   e

48 DIFFICULTY ✪✪✪✪✪✪✪✪✪✪ ⟨**4**⟩ Minutes

On petri dish a there are currently 5,000 bacteria that produce another 250 bacteria per hour. On petri dish b there are currently 12,000 bacteria, but 100 bacteria die per hour. When will both dishes have an identical bacteria population?

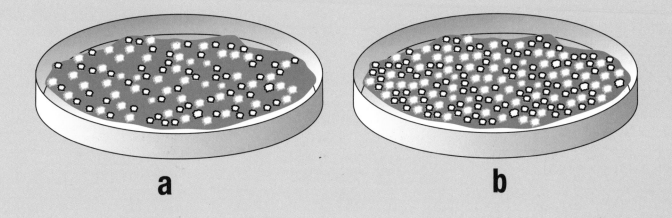

a   b

49 DIFFICULTY ✪✪✪✪✪✪✪✪✪✪ ⏱ 5 Minutes

Can you fit these numbers into the grid? One number has already been inserted to help you get started.

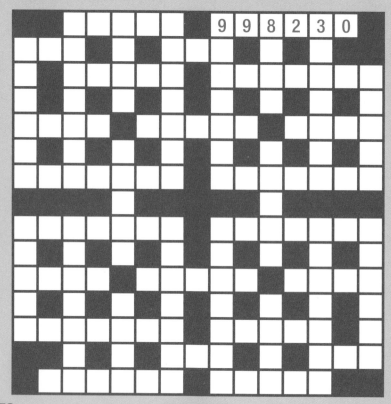

3 DIGITS	5 DIGITS	7 DIGITS
376	17686	1266562
579	21019	1745427
798	33644	2137924
964	46399	2735436
	59575	3675684
4 DIGITS	66796	4487579
1560	74716	5997674
2258	84664	6337004
3065	94955	6727751
4696	99145	7178438
5862		7912329
7213	**6 DIGITS**	8148431
8024	546262	9467952
9332	695591	9945593
	782758	
	998230	

50 DIFFICULTY ✪✪✪✪✪✪✪✪✪✪

 **7** Minutes

Can you crack the safe? First decide which of the 14 statements given are false, then shade out the areas on the combination lock that are labeled with the letters of those false statements (so if you think statement A is false, shade out area A). The remaining lit segments will give you the digital combination required.

Hint: four of the statements are false.

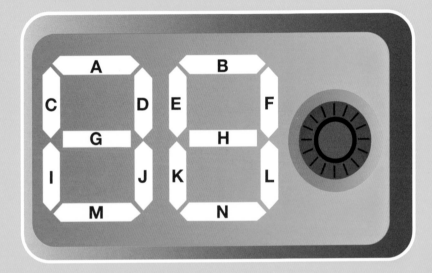

A. There are a dozen dozens in a gross.
B. 39 is a prime number.
C. 111 x 111 = 12,321.
D. 50 divided by 0.5 equals 25.
E. The total score you get from rolling two standard dice is 7, on average.
F. The positive square root of 121 is 11.
G. (1/2) x (2/3) x (3/4) x (4/5) = 1/5.
H. There are 1,440 minutes in a typical day.
I. If the digits of a whole number add up to 9, the number is divisible by 9.
J. "Threescore years and ten" equals 70 years.
K. If P x Q = Q, then P must be 1.
L. If two angles in a triangle are 36 and 54 degrees, the third angle is a right angle.
M. In Roman numerals, I + V + X + L + C + D + M = 1,666.
N. The cube of 5 is 225.

51 DIFFICULTY ○○○○○○○○○○

8 Minutes

Five owners brought their dragsters to race. Can you match each racer with his last name, name the cars, and find out each car's speed?

1. Steve's Blisterine wasn't the fastest, and neither was the dragster owned by Zak Dupris.
2. Van Happs's Hot Stuff was 25 mph slower than one car, but only 10 mph slower than Jackson.
3. Marty was second quickest—20 mph quicker than Chicken Speed.
4. Fast and Loose wasn't the quickest, but it was quicker than Bubba.
5. Schwartz was quicker than Delaney.

	Last name					mph					Name				
	Jackson	Delaney	Schwartz	Dupris	Van Happs	235	240	250	255	265	Rock Racer	Blisterine	Hot Stuff	Chicken Speed	Fast and Loose
Steve															
Zak															
Bubba															
Marty															
Kate															
Rock Racer															
Blisterine															
Hot Stuff															
Chicken Speed															
Fast and Loose															
235															
240															
250															
255															
265															

52 DIFFICULTY ○○○○○○○○○○

4 Minutes

Make a calculation totaling the figure on the right by inserting the four mathematical operators (+, −, ÷, x) between the numbers shown.

The mathematical operators can be in any order, and one of them has been used twice.

| 4 | | 6 | | 5 | | 2 | | 7 | | 3 | = | 8 |

53 DIFFICULTY ✪✪✪✪✪✪✪✪☆☆

 **8** Minutes

Make your way from top left to bottom right in this number maze. You may only move to calculations that total either one more or one less than the previous sum.

22 ÷ 11	24 ÷ 6	36 ÷ 6	63 ÷ 9	3 + 3
34 ÷ 34	11 − 8	5 x 1	2 + 1	4 + 4
11 − 9	20 ÷ 4	0 + 4	11 − 6	2 + 5
3 x 1	3 + 2	5 ÷ 1	2 x 5	24 ÷ 3
36 ÷ 9	21 − 8	3 x 4	13 − 4	22 − 13
7 x 2	25 ÷ 5	8 + 3	70 ÷ 10	18 ÷ 2
1 + 6	3 x 5	23 − 10	6 + 5	16 − 6
21 ÷ 3	21 − 7	2 + 11	39 ÷ 3	5 + 9
4 x 2	3 x 3	2 x 5	6 x 2	5 x 3
28 ÷ 4	5 x 2	5 + 8	2 x 8	27 − 12

54 DIFFICULTY ✪✪✪✪✪✪✪✪✪✪

30 Minutes

Can you keep on the right track with this numeropic? Refer to the instructions on how to do this puzzle on page 15 if you need any help.

Column clues (top):

											2		3														
		1	1		2	2	2	1	4	2	3	6								3							
	13	1	1	7	2	4	3	3	3	1	5	6	2	3	2	1	14	3	3	5	3						
	13	2	13	7	2	7	2	1	1	1	2	1	1	2	8	7	13	2	5	5	2	5	6				
4	1	13	2	1	3	3	2	2	2	2	2	2	3	3	2	2	2	2	2	3	3	1	2	6	3	3	2
13	1	11	4	2	1	2	2	1	2	1	1	1	2	1	2	2	1	2	1	2	1	2	1	2	4	14	1	3
1	2	2	2	1	1	2	3	2	2	1	1	1	2	2	3	2	1	1	2	2	2	2	2	1	2	2	2	1	1

Row clues (left):

- 7
- 8
- 4 3
- 3
- 3
- 8
- 4 10
- 6 10
- 4 2 1
- 4 1 2 1
- 4 3 2 2
- 4 5 2 1
- 19 1
- 20 2
- 27
- 10 11
- 9 10
- 10 11
- 26
- 1 1
- 1 26 1
- 30
- 1 2 2 2 2 2 1
- 2 1 1 1 1 1 1 2
- 1 18 1
- 1 2 1 1 2 1 1 2 1
- 1 1 1 1 1 1 1
- 2 2 2
- 30
- 3 3 3 3 3

55 DIFFICULTY ✪✪✪✪✪✪✪✪✪✪

5 Minutes

The number 295617 appears just once in this grid and occurs in a straight line, running either backward or forward in a horizontal, vertical, or diagonal direction. Can you locate it?

```
      2 9 5
    6 1 7 2 9 5 6
    1 7 2 9 5 6 7 7 2
    9 5 6 1 7 2 6 7 5 9 1
  2 2 7 2 9 5 9 1 2 7 5 7 2
  7 9 9 9 6 2 5 2 6 9 6 6 1
9 2 5 6 1 7 2 6 1 2 5 1 9 5 2
2 5 9 6 1 9 5 5 6 9 2 9 5 1 9
2 9 5 1 5 6 9 7 7 5 6 7 2 6 5
  9 7 6 5 2 7 2 1 7 6 1 7 2
  7 9 1 2 6 1 1 6 1 5 6 9 5
    7 5 9 1 2 9 5 6 7 9 2
    2 6 7 6 5 9 9 1 9
      7 2 5 9 2 9 2
        9 2 5
```

56 DIFFICULTY ✪✪✪✪✪✪✪☆☆☆  **7** Minutes

Each block is equal to the sum of the two numbers beneath it. Can you find all the missing numbers?

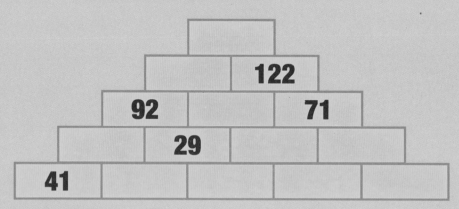

56 DIFFICULTY ✪☆☆☆✪☆✪✪✪✪  **8** Minutes

Five workers at a candy factory all have different jobs on different lines. Can you match each first name to a last name, a product, and a job?

	Toggle	Duffy	Button	Hopper	Dorrit	Packing	Quality control	Wrapping	Orders	Tasting	Fudge	Truffles	Mints	Caramels	Lollipops
Deborah															
Diane															
Brenda															
Bob															
Brian															
Fudge															
Truffles															
Mints															
Caramels															
Lollipops															
Packing															
Quality Control															
Wrapping															
Orders															
Tasting															

1. Mr. or Mrs. Dorrit works with fudge and not with Brenda.
2. Diane Toggle doesn't wrap and she doesn't work with mints or truffles.
3. Bob in orders doesn't deal with caramels.
4. No one with a first name that begins with "B" works in quality control.
5. There are no women in lollipops and no men in mints.
6. The truffle taster is a woman, but she isn't Deborah Duffy.
7. Bob doesn't work in lollipops.
8. Mr. or Mrs. Button works in packing. Caramels are not wrapped.

58 DIFFICULTY ✪✪✪✪✪✪✪✪✪✪

6 Minutes

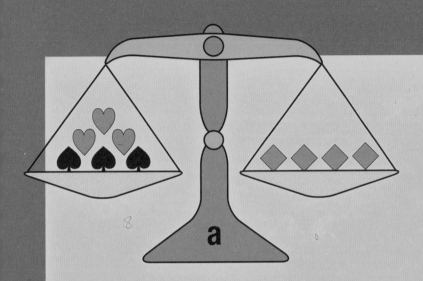

Given that scales a
and b balance
perfectly, how many
hearts are needed to
balance scale c?

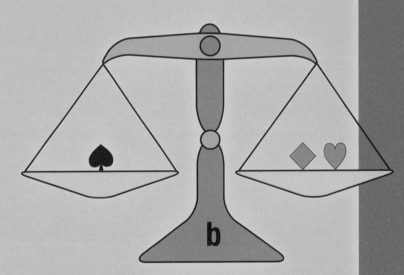

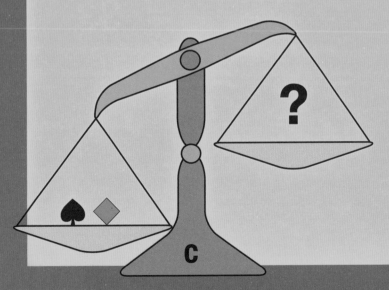

5 Minutes

Each row and column contains the same numbers and signs, but they are arranged in a different order each time. Find the correct order to arrive at the final totals shown.

9	+	6	x	3	–	7	=	38
							=	28
							=	12
							=	33
=		=		=		=		
43		50		84		48		

60 DIFFICULTY ✪✪✪✪✪✪✪✩✩✩  **Minute**

We've given the cards shown here different values, so that an ace = 1, jack = 11, queen = 12, and king = 13, while all other cards have the same value as their numbers. Study this arrangement of cards carefully for one minute, then see if you can answer the questions on page 54.

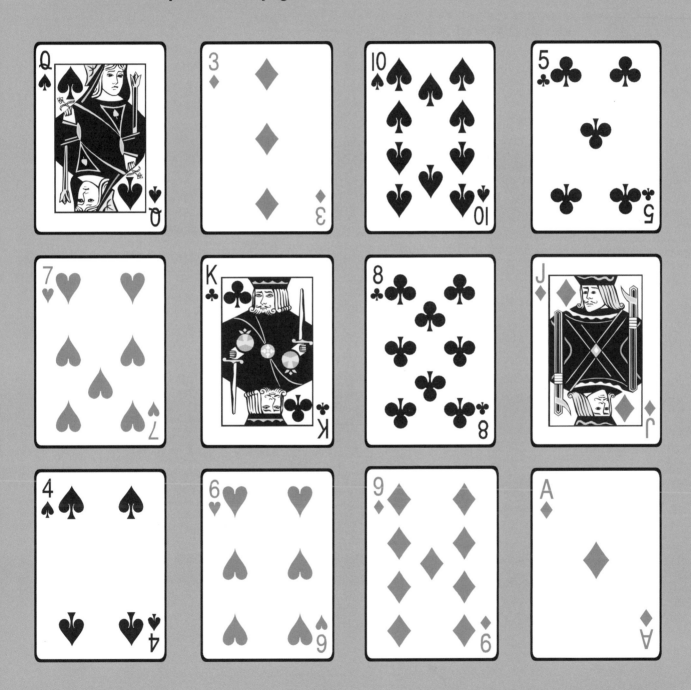

[60] DIFFICULTY ✪✪✪✪✪✪✪✪✪✪  **5** Minutes

Can you answer these questions about the puzzle on page 53 without looking back?

1. Which suit is the king?

2. Which number does not appear?

3. What is the lowest total value of four cards in a row?

4. What is the lowest total value of three cards in a column?

5. Which card is directly to the left of the 9 of diamonds?

6. What is the total value of the four corner cards?

7. Which suit is the ten?

8. Which card is directly above the 9 of diamonds?

61 DIFFICULTY ✪✪✪✪✪✪✪✪✪✪  **4** Minutes

Make a calculation totaling the figure on the right by inserting the four mathematical operators (+, −, ÷, x) between the numbers shown.

They can be inserted in any order, and one of them has been used twice.

| 10 | | 7 | | 11 | | 4 | | 8 | | 12 | = | 19 |

62 DIFFICULTY ✪✪✪✪✪✪✪✪✪✪

5 Minutes

Can you fit these numbers into the grid? One number has already been inserted to help you get started.

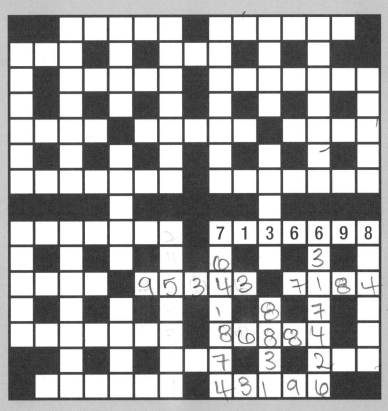

3 DIGITS
247
264
413
487

4 DIGITS
2528
3248
6283
6973
7184
8145
8831
9281

5 DIGITS
21643
28634
35138
38626
43196
54332
84461
86884
91798
95343

6 DIGITS
396889
442955
813158
895314

7 DIGITS
1582989
2413379
2757941
3396839
3397591
4845548
5558199
5597831
6317426
6489451
7136698
7641874
8744372
9159129

63 DIFFICULTY ✪✪✪✪✪✪✩✩✩✩  3 Minutes

Take a close look at the patterned shields below. Which one is the odd one out?

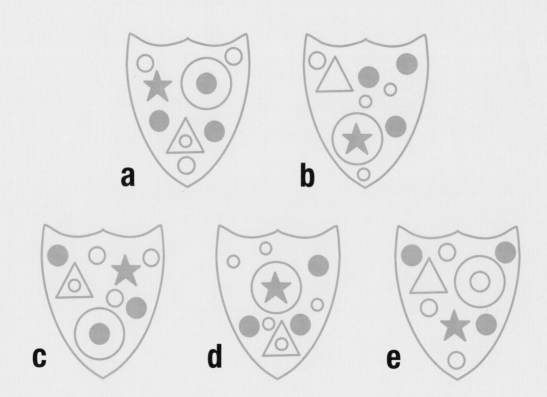

a   b

c   d   e

64 DIFFICULTY ✪✪✪✪✪✪✪✩✩✩  2 Minutes

What number comes next?

749326

239746

479236

65 DIFFICULTY ✪✪✪✪✪✪✪✪✪✪

Minutes

The number 472596 appears just once in this grid and occurs in a straight line, running either backward or forward in a horizontal, vertical, or diagonal direction; however, as you can see, the numbers are reversed! Can you locate it?

66 DIFFICULTY ✪✪✪✪✪✩✩✩✩✩

For this game, you will need three coins or counters for each player. The first player chooses a circle on the board to place the first piece. The second player then does the same. Play continues in the usual manner until all the players have played their pieces.

The aim is to get your three pieces in a horizontal, vertical, or diagonal line. If there is no winner after the first six opening moves, the first player chooses any coin and slides it along a line to any available adjacent circle. The second player takes a turn and so on. The first player to make a line of three wins the game.

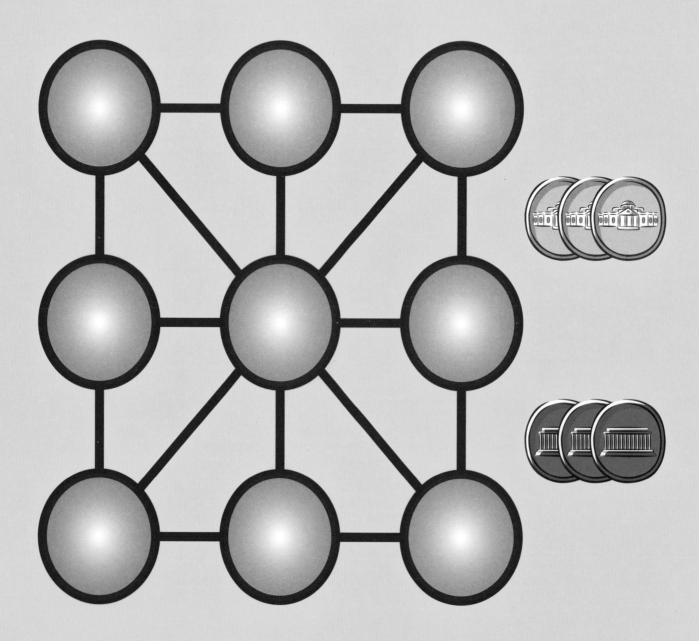

67 DIFFICULTY ✪✪✪✪✪✪✪✪✪✪  Minutes

Can you steam through this numeropic in record time? If you need any help in completing this puzzle, refer to the instructions on page 15.

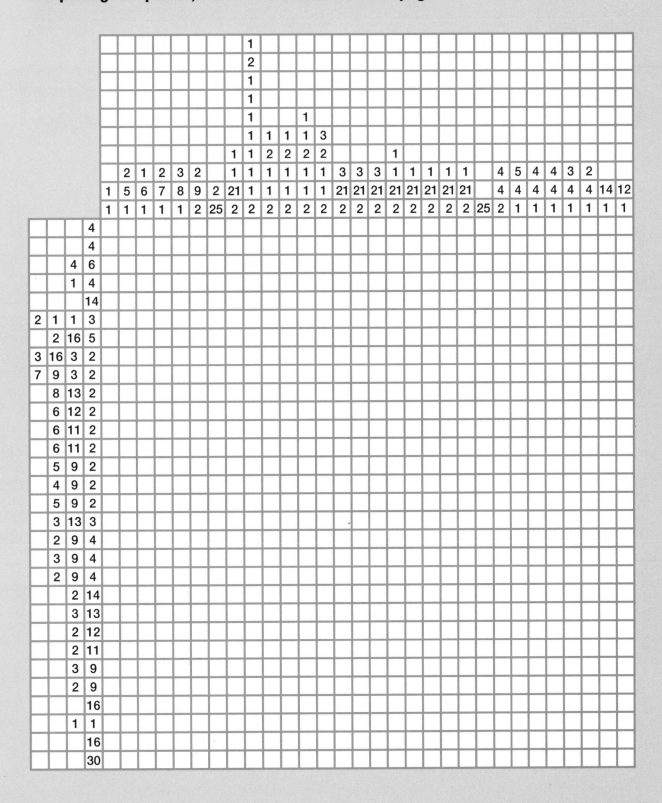

68 DIFFICULTY ✪✪✪✪✪✪✪✪✪✪  **4** Minutes

Make a calculation totaling the figure on the right by inserting the four mathematical operators (+, −, ÷, x) between the numbers shown.

They can be inserted in any order, and one of them has been used twice.

| 20 | | 14 | | 9 | | 6 | | 18 | | 3 | = | 44 |

69 DIFFICULTY ✪✪✪✪✪✪✪✪✪✪  **3** Minutes

Use your powers of logic to determine what number comes next in the sequence below.

36, 91, 21, 51, 82, 12, 42, ?

70 DIFFICULTY  5 Minutes

Each block in this number pyramid is equal to the sum of the two numbers beneath it. Can you deduce all the missing numbers?

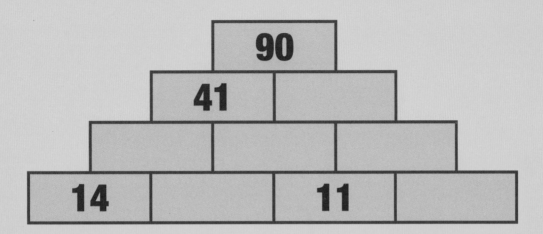

71 DIFFICULTY  5 Minutes

If you saw these somewhat eccentric clocks on an office wall, what would be the logical time for GEORGETOWN?

72 DIFFICULTY ✪✪✪✪✩✩✩✩✩ ⏱ **5** Minutes

Which of the four boxed figures (a, b, c, or d) completes the set?

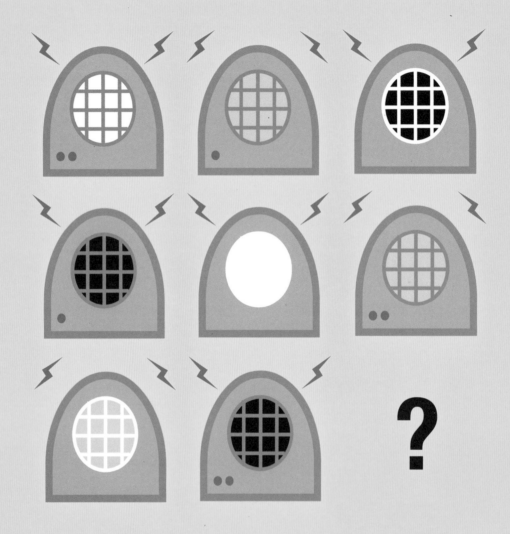

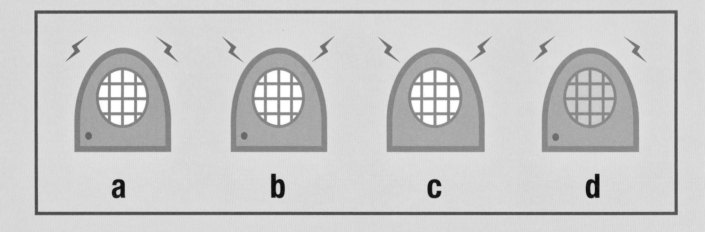

a   b   c   d

73 DIFFICULTY ✪✪✪✪✪✪✪✪✪  **Minutes**

Place the loose tiles into the grid and ensure that:

* no row or column contains three tiles of the same color, and
* each row, column, and main diagonal adds up to 18.

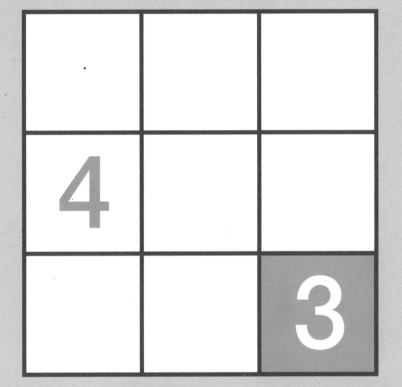

 **5** Minutes

Can you fit these numbers into the grid? One number has already been inserted to help you get started.

| 2 | 3 | 7 | 4 | 5 |

3 DIGITS
197
318
795
816

4 DIGITS
1637
2596
3827
4622
5962
6241
8913
9677

5 DIGITS
12382
~~23745~~
39544
49833
54143
63416
77456
81758
82632
97188

6 DIGITS
151241
268298
663215
979198

7 DIGITS
1122752
1538888
2212918
3785942
3791668
4329272
5838986
5853511
6197375
7673189
8114462
8456616
9612239
9873892

75 DIFFICULTY ✪✪✪✪✪✪✪☆☆☆  **1** Minute

Study these dice for one minute, then see if you can answer the questions on page 66.

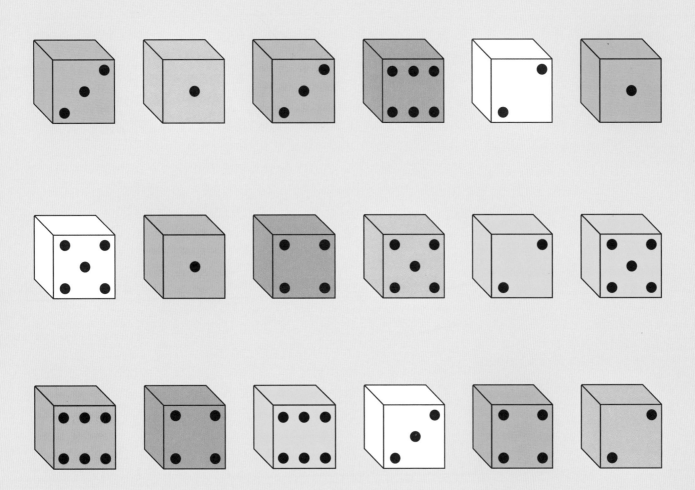

76 DIFFICULTY ✪✪✪✪✪✪✪☆☆☆  **2** Minutes

A security guard is working a long night shift. At ten past one in the morning, he makes his first patrol. He patrols another four times at 70-minute intervals. He can then rest for a few hours before the patrol just after ten o'clock. He completes two more patrols with 70-minute gaps before clocking off at lunchtime. What superstition does he have?

[75] DIFFICULTY ✪✪✪✪✪✪✪✪✪✪✪ **3** Minutes

Can you answer these questions about the dice on page 65 without looking back?

1. What is the color of the die directly below the white die that has five spots?
2. What is the sum total of the number of spots on the two most central dice?
3. What is the color of the die directly to the left of the blue die with two spots?
4. What is the color of the die directly above the orange die with one spot?
5. What is the sum total of the number of spots on all of the pink dice?
6. What are the colors of the three dice that have only one spot?
7. Only two dice of the same color are horizontally adjacent to one another: what is the sum total of the number of spots on these two dice?
8. Only two dice are identical: what is the color of these two dice?

77 DIFFICULTY ✪✪✪✪✪✪✪✪✪✪✪ **3** Minutes

Which box below should replace the question mark in the above sequence?

a   b   c   d   e   f   g

78 DIFFICULTY ✪✪✪✪✪✪✪✪✪✪  Minutes

This puzzle uses the 16 face cards and aces from all four suits of a standard deck of cards. Complete the grid so that no row or column contains two cards of the same denomination or suit.

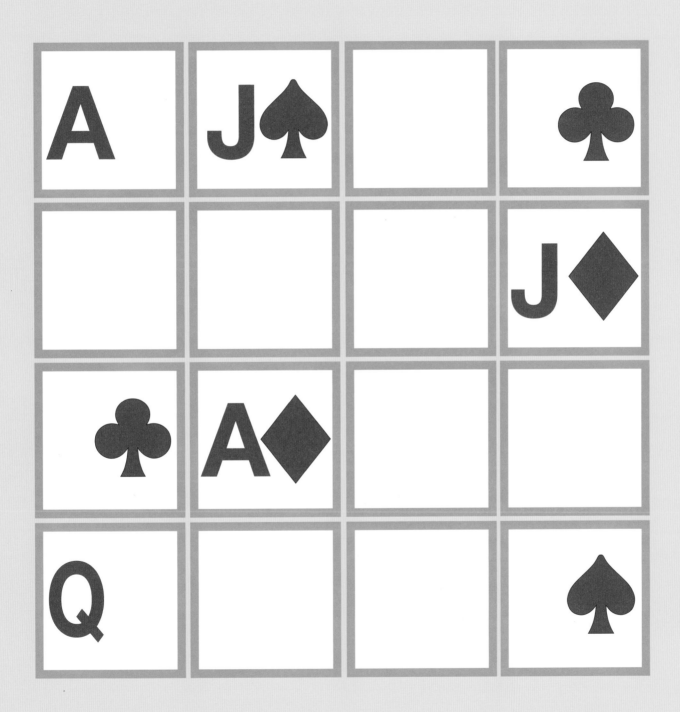

79 DIFFICULTY ✪✪✪✪✪✪✪✪✪✪ 6 Minutes

Can you crack the safe? First decide which of the 14 statements given are false. Then shade out the areas on the combination lock that are labeled with the letters of those false statements (so if you think statement A is false, shade out area A). The remaining lit segments will give you the digital combination required.

Hint: five of the statements are false.

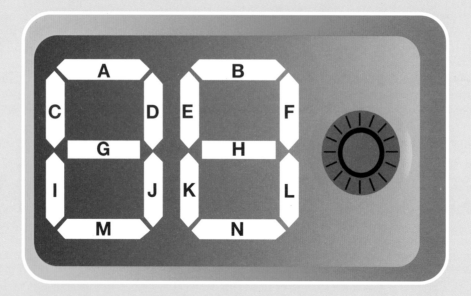

A. Ronald Reagan was the 40th president of the United States.
B. IQ stands for Intelligence Quota.
C. In architecture, a campanile is a bell tower.
D. In medieval times, a knight's glove was called a gauntlet.
E. The first Boeing 747 jumbo jet flew in February 1959.
F. A force 12 storm on the Beaufort scale is a hurricane.
G. Clint Eastwood won the Best Director Oscar for *Unforgiven* in 1992.
H. A lepidopterist collects coins.
I. Montezuma II was the last emperor of the Aztecs.
J. Limestone and chalk are forms of calcium carbonate.
K. Omega is the fourth letter of the Greek alphabet.
L. The real name of Batman is Bruce Wayne.
M. El Cid and Macbeth were born in the same century.
N. *Cygnus cygnus* is the Latin classification for the raven.

80 DIFFICULTY ✪✪✪✪✪✪☆✪☆☆    **4** Minutes

Complete the calculation totaling the figure on the right by inserting the four mathematical operators (+, −, ÷, x) between the numbers shown.

The mathematical operators can be in any order, and one of them has been used twice.

| 44 | | 11 | | 57 | | 39 | | 13 | | 86 | = | 200 |

81 DIFFICULTY ✪✪✪✪✪✪✪☆☆☆    **6** Minutes

Take the cards around the outside of the grid and place them so that each horizontal row contains cards of six different values and each vertical column contains cards of four different values and four different suits. No card should be placed either horizontally or vertically next to one of the same color. The values of the cards are as per their numbers. Cards already in place should not be moved.

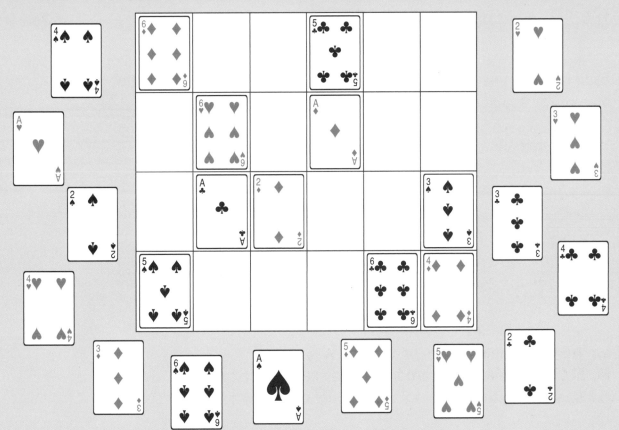

82 DIFFICULTY ✪✪✪✪✪✪✪✪✪✪ ⏱ 2 Minutes

Which number is the odd one out?

6839

7421

8243

2471

4283

3869

9263

83 DIFFICULTY ✪✪✪✪✪✪✪✪✪✪ ⏱ 5 Minutes

Each block in this especially difficult number pyramid is equal to the sum of the two numbers beneath it. Find the missing numbers.

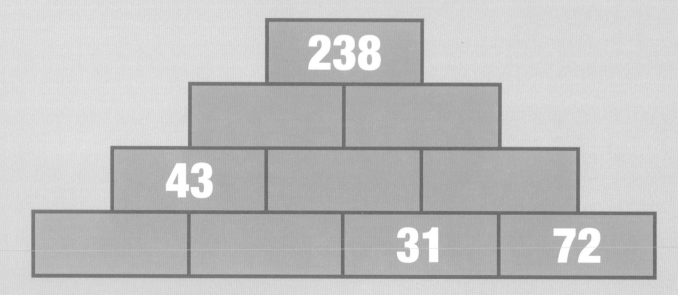

238

43

31   72

84 DIFFICULTY ✪✪✪✪✪✪✩✩✩✩  **3** Minutes

3682497

is to

9738642

and

285417

is to

751842

and

7186293

is to…

?

85 DIFFICULTY ✪✪✪✪✪✪✪✪☆☆  **5** Minutes

Each of the blocks in this challenging number pyramid is equal to the sum of the two numbers beneath it. Can you find all of the missing numbers?

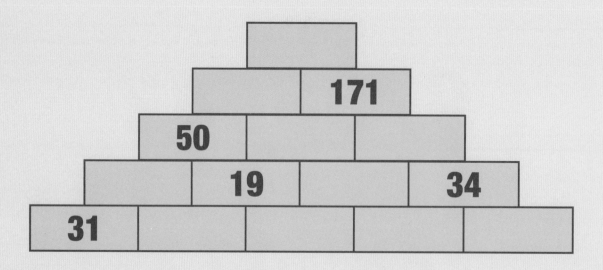

86 DIFFICULTY ✪✪✪✪✪✪✪✪✪✪  **4** Minutes

Make a calculation totaling the figure on the right by inserting the four mathematical operators (+, −, ÷, x) between the numbers shown.

They can be inserted in any order, and one of them has been used twice.

| 70 | | 86 | | 13 | | 66 | | 4 | | 27 | = | 171 |

87 DIFFICULTY ✪✪✪✪✪✪✪☆☆☆

 **10** Minutes

Five soccer players, playing in different positions, scored a varying number of goals for their teams. Can you match each first name with a last name, a team, a position, and a number of goals scored?

	Callan	Brady	Best	Charlton	Hughes	City	Town	Rangers	United	Rovers	Right Wing	Center Forward	Defender	Midfield	Left Wing	1	2	3	4	5
Wayne																				
David																					
Paul																					
Darius																					
Emile																					
1															
2															
3															
4															
5															
Right Wing										
Center Forward										
Defender										
Midfield										
Left Wing										
City					
Town					
Rangers					
United					
Rovers					

Goals

1. **Wayne Brady isn't a midfielder or a center forward. He scored more goals than Darius.**
2. **Rovers' Charlton scored more than Brady.**
3. **The Rangers' center forward scored two less than the Rovers' player.**
4. **Paul, playing for United, scored one more than David.**
5. **Hughes got four. He isn't a winger.**
6. **Emile, the left winger, scored two more than the center forward and one less than the Town player.**
7. **Callan got one less than the City defender.**

88 DIFFICULTY ✪✪✪✪✪✪✪✪✪✪  4 Minutes

Make a calculation totaling the figure on the right by inserting the four mathematical operators (+, −, ÷, x) between the numbers shown.

They can be inserted in any order, and one of them has been used twice.

| 14 | | 5 | | 33 | | 19 | | 4 | | 15 | = | 36 |

89 DIFFICULTY ✪✪✪✪✪✪✪✪✪✪  2 Minutes

Which number below is the odd one out?

3984 7456

1203 7896

5032 3527

90 DIFFICULTY ✪✪✪✪✪✪✪✪✪✪  Minutes

Given that scales a and b balance perfectly, how many spoons are needed to balance scale c?

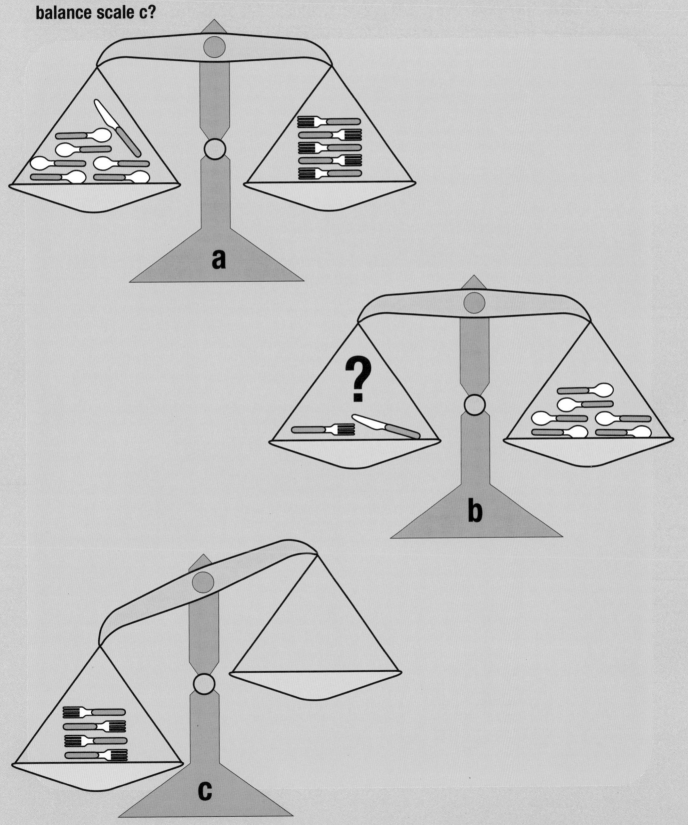

91 DIFFICULTY ✪✪✪✪✪✩✩✩✩  5 Minutes

This puzzle uses the 16 face cards and aces from all four suits from a standard deck of cards. Complete the grid by adding suits and face names so that no row, column, or main diagonal contains two cards of the same denomination or suit.

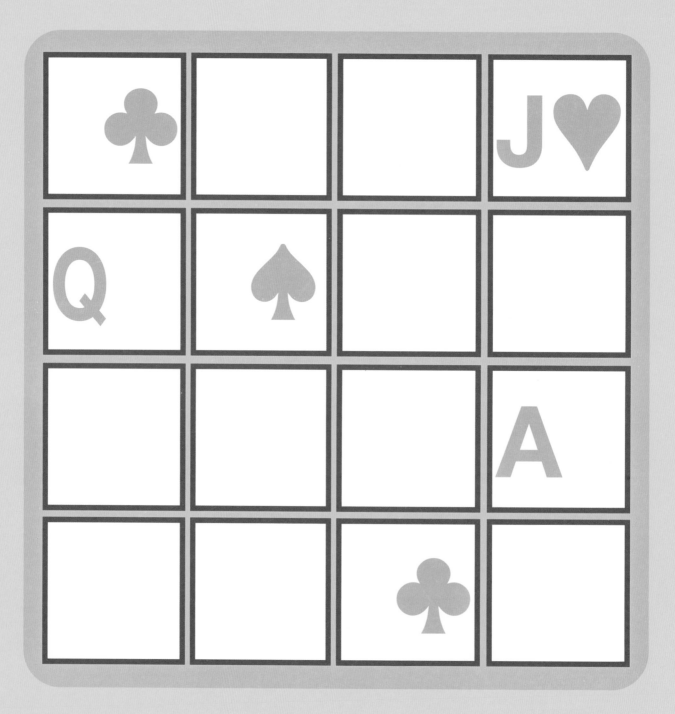

92 DIFFICULTY ✪✪✪✪✪✩✩✩✩✩  Minutes

The following message has been encoded using a typewriter:

Yjr vpfr eptf od s voyu om Mre Uptl dysyr, ejovj od frdvtonrf sd s nodpm om yjr ID.

Look at the typewriter layout carefully and see if you can unscramble the sentence. Then figure out the seven-letter answer to the question it poses.

93 DIFFICULTY ✪✪✪✩✩✩✩✩✩✩  Minutes

What number comes next?

3749216
629473
37496
?

94 DIFFICULTY  **3** Minutes

The numbers 2468 and 13579 each appear just once in this grid and occur in straight lines, running either backward or forward in a horizontal, vertical, or diagonal direction. Can you locate them both?

95 DIFFICULTY ✪✪✪✪✪☆☆☆☆☆ ⏱ 5 Minutes

Can you fit these numbers into the grid? One number has already been inserted to help you get started.

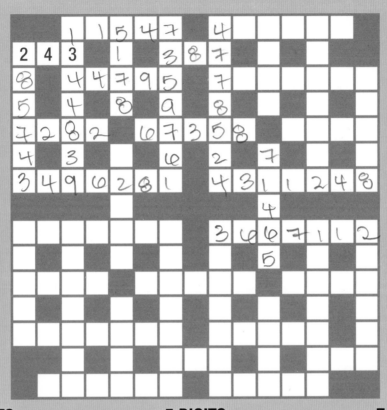

3 DIGITS

~~888~~
~~88~~
544
906

4 DIGITS

1855
3196
3327
4282
5178
~~4288~~
8924
9415

5 DIGITS

~~88888~~
23365
24444
32945
~~88888~~
52658
~~88888~~
~~88888~~
84394
92274

6 DIGITS

~~888888~~
444838
682584
735586

7 DIGITS

~~8888888~~ ✓
2688778
~~8888888~~
~~8888888~~
~~8888888~~
~~8888888~~
5611418
6589594
7359761
7585615
8148854
8824138
9299342
9569677

96 DIFFICULTY ✪✪✪✪✪✪✫✫✫✫  **3** Minutes

4837 is to **715**

and

6293 is to **155**

and

5978 is to **?**

97 DIFFICULTY ✪✪✪✪✪✪✫✫✫✫  **7** Minutes

Remove five cards from the grid and replace them in different positions so that the values of the cards in each row, column, and long diagonal line of cards totals exactly 25. The value of each card is as per its number.

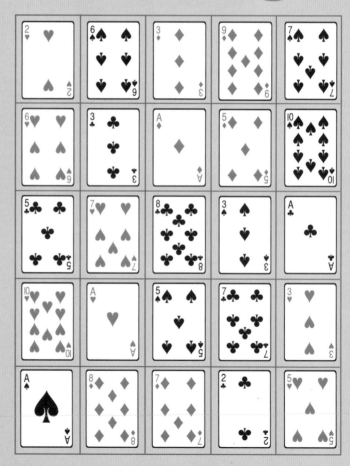

98 DIFFICULTY ✪✪✪✪✪✪✪☆☆  10 Minutes

Five children entered five different events at the school fair and finished in five different positions. Can you match each child to his or her last name, the event each entered, and the venue at which the event was held?

1. Bobby Macfie played marbles. There were only three competitors in the event and it wasn't on the soccer field.

2. The 3rd place finisher in the common room wasn't a girl.

3. The 4th place finisher in the hopscotch wasn't a girl or named Stuart.

4. The child who played Hacky Sack, not a Stuart, was placed higher than the child who jumped rope.

5. Wendy was in the playground. Young Macdonald and Macfie were not.

6. Betsy Campbell didn't win her event, which wasn't hopscotch, and wasn't held in the cafeteria.

7. Billy came first, but not in the Hacky Sack or marbles, and not on the soccer field.

8. The jump-rope event was held in the quad and was won by a girl.

9. The Hacky Sack competitor's first name didn't begin with "B" and he/she wasn't in the cafeteria or the common room.

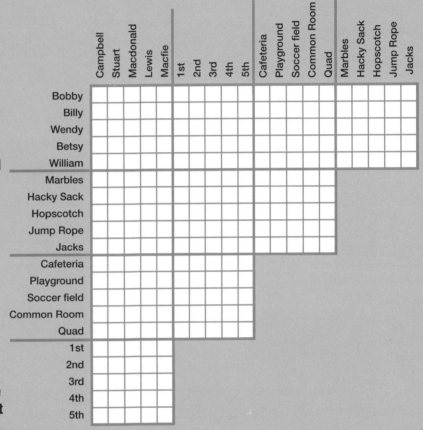

99 DIFFICULTY ✪✪✪✪✪☆☆☆☆  5 Minutes

Make a calculation totaling the figure on the right by inserting the four mathematical operators (+, −, ÷, x) between the numbers shown.

They can be inserted in any order, and one of them has been used twice.

| 13 | | 27 | | 10 | | 15 | | 11 | | 9 | = | 72 |

100 DIFFICULTY ✪✪✪✪✪✩✩✩✩✩  **6** Minutes

Each row and column contains exactly the same numbers and signs, but they are arranged in a different order each time. Find the correct order to arrive at the final totals shown.

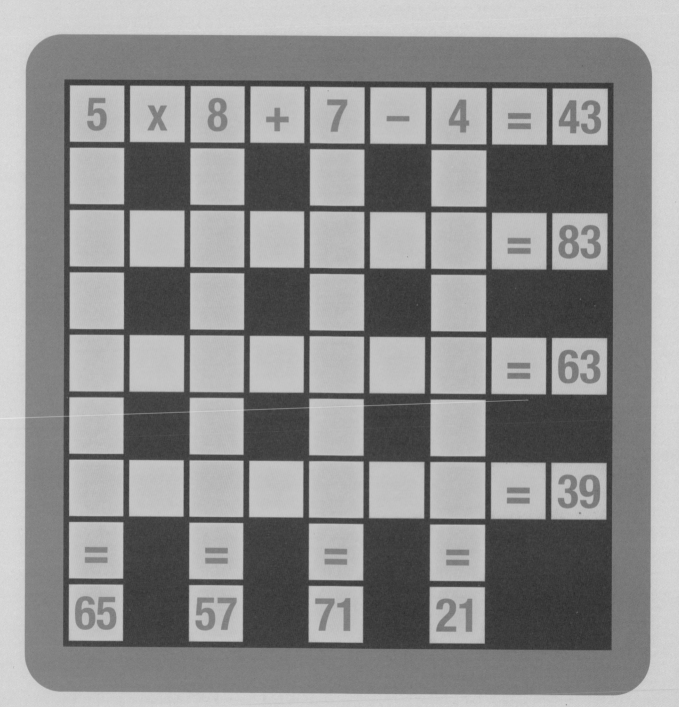

101 DIFFICULTY ✪✪✪✪✪✪✪✩✩✩

 Minutes

There is only one logical way to get from a to b visiting all the patterns in this code maze. Can you find the hidden sequence by figuring out how the pattern changes from start to finish? Your lines may cross but you may not use any path or corner more than once.

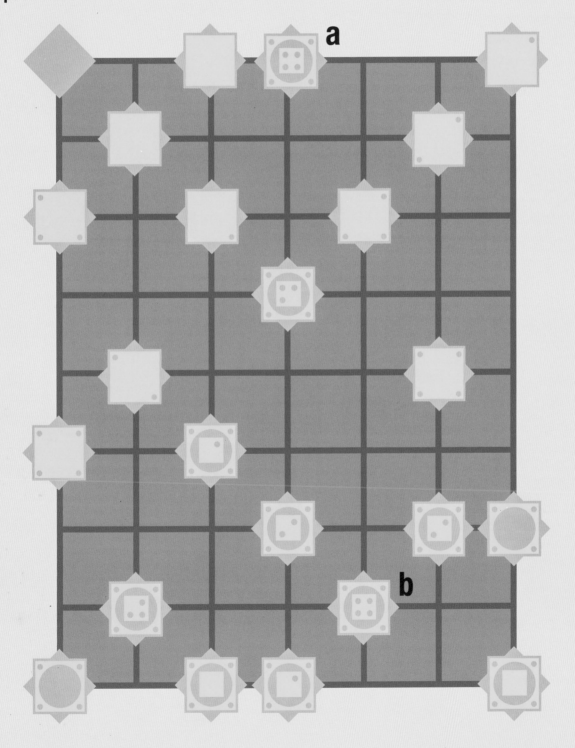

102 DIFFICULTY ✪✪✪✪✪☆☆☆☆☆

This is an interesting word variation of a popular logical game. It requires two players or teams, which we shall call the Setter and the Guesser. The Setter chooses a common five-letter English word that has all different letters. The Guesser then writes down his or her first guess as to what that word is.

The Setter helps the Guesser by drawing:
* a circle around correct letters that are in the correct place, and
* a square around correct letters that are in the wrong position.

In the example shown, the Guesser has taken five words to deduce the Setter's word. Players can now swap roles and see who can guess their opponent's word the quickest.

Beginners to this game might like to give their opponents the first letter of the word so that the opponents can begin their guesses with a purpose.

1. ASKED
2. CHASM
3. CIGAR
4. LOGIC
5. MAGIC

103 DIFFICULTY ✪✪✪✪✪✪✪✪✪✪  **Minutes**

Which of the boxed figures (a, b, c, or d) completes the set?

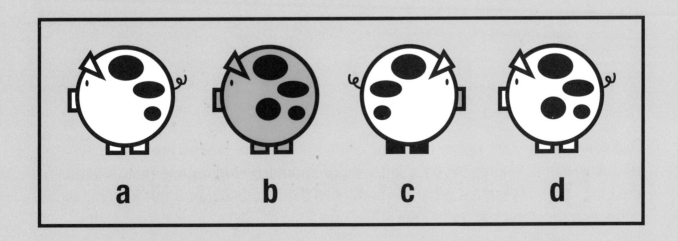

a   b   c   d

104 DIFFICULTY ✪✪✪✪✪✪✪✪✪✪  **3** Minutes

2634

7529

18

24 28

5816

Which two numbers, one in the group above and one
in the group below, are the odd ones out?

4275 20

1698

16 23 9865

105 DIFFICULTY ✪✪✪✪✪✪✪✪✪✪  **3** Minutes

Two running partners follow the same route at the same time at the same pace.
However, one measures his pace in terms of minutes taken for one mile, whereas
the other uses kilometers per hour. Curiously, both statistics turn out to give the
same number. How fast were they going? Assume 8 kilometers equals 5 miles.

106 DIFFICULTY ✪✪✪✪✪✪✪✪☆  **7** Minutes

Each block in this difficult number pyramid is equal to the sum of the two numbers beneath it. Can you find all the missing numbers?

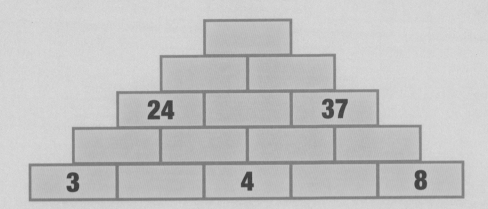

107 DIFFICULTY ✪✪✪✪✪☆☆☆☆  **3** Minutes

What numbers should replace the question marks in each line?

74 55 36 ??

98 67 36 ??

108 DIFFICULTY ✪✪✪✪✪✪✪☆☆☆    5 Minutes

Can you fit these numbers into the grid? One number has already been inserted to help you get started.

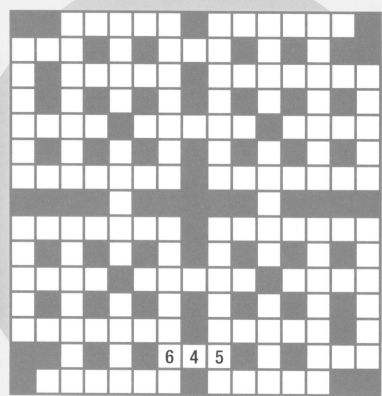

3 DIGITS	5 DIGITS	7 DIGITS
215	13124	1248958
261	14689	1638323
~~645~~	16877	2162177
728	22181	2173553
	24745	2374856
4 DIGITS	33621	3128791
1727	39713	3819862
2365	54366	4628248
4696	55923	5141821
5887	59228	6965163
6614		7429496
7521	**6 DIGITS**	8139288
9843	715785	8447319
9947	761584	9372633
	861383	
	861897	

109 DIFFICULTY ✪✪✪✪✪✪✪✪✪✪

 **30** Minutes

Blaze a trail to solve this numeropic. If you find it useful, refer to page 15 for instructions on how to complete this puzzle.

Column clues (top):

									1																		
								1	1				1										2				
								1	1	6	3		1	1									2				
			2					1	1	6	9		1	1	4	4			9	9	3	4	4				
	5	2	5	10	10		1	3	2	1	1	3	13	20	10	10	11	1	4	6	4	3	2	7	5		
1	4	5	1	2	5	3	3	13		14	10	8	1	1	2	3	10	4	3	4	2	11	11	12	4	4	2	2	3
1	1	1	1	1	1	1	1	2	3	20	1	1	1	1	1	1	1	2	3	4	1	1	1	1	1	1	1	1	1

Row clues (left):

				4	2
			4	2	2
		8	2	2	2
		1	2	5	2
				5	8
				4	6
			1	3	3
			3	7	3
	5	1	4	1	3
		2	4	8	3
	9	1	4	1	2
			10	5	4
		4	6	8	5
		2	8	9	2
			7	10	2
			7	11	2
			6	9	2
			7	8	1
				7	8
				6	8
				12	6
			6	4	6
		2	2	4	6
		1	2	4	5
		1	2	4	4
		2	1	2	4
		3	1	2	2
			2	2	1
				3	3
					30

110 DIFFICULTY ✪✪✪✪✪✪✪✪✪✪  **Minutes**

Can you place the tiles into the magic grid so that their numbers lie on the correct colored squares, and each row, column, and main diagonal adds up to 34?

111 DIFFICULTY ✪✪✪✪✪✪✪✪✪✪  **5** Minutes

Each row and column contains the same numbers and signs, but they are arranged in a different order each time. Find the correct order to arrive at the final totals shown.

13	+	12	x	25	–	16	=	609
							=	121
							=	147
							=	336
=		=		=		=		
416		180		377		713		

112 DIFFICULTY ✪✪✪✪✪✪✪✪✪✪  3 Minutes

Which pair of numbers is the odd one out? Why?

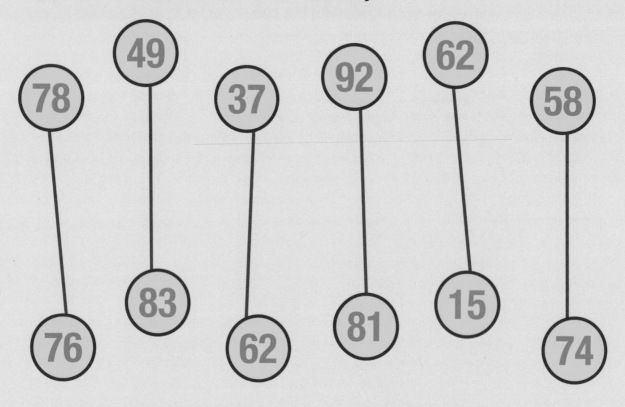

113 DIFFICULTY ✪✪✪✪✪✪✪✪✪✪ 2 Minutes

An analog clock has fallen on the floor but is still operational. There is no way of seeing which way up the clock should go, but your perfect eyesight can tell that the minute and hour hands are pointing precisely toward two of the 60 tick marks on the clock face. Furthermore, the hands are exactly one tick apart.

So…what time is it?

114 DIFFICULTY ✪✪✪✪✪✪✩✩✩  **3** **Minutes**

7	9	3	6
5	8	7	2
8	4	3	6
5	8	2	9

is to:

4	9	4	6
9	5	9	8
3	2	6	2
8	7	3	7

as

7	2	6	4
3	8	9	7
6	5	8	3
5	4	5	6

is to:

3	6	3	5
4	5	8	2
3	8	7	8
8	3	5	6

a

4	7	3	6
6	9	8	5
2	8	5	4
7	3	6	5

b

4	7	2	6
5	4	9	3
4	9	8	7
7	2	6	5

c

8	3	7	3
4	7	8	6
7	4	9	2
4	5	4	5

d

115 DIFFICULTY ✪✪✪✪✪✪✪✪✪✪  **6** Minutes

Can you crack the safe? First decide which of the 14 statements given are false, then shade out the areas on the combination lock that are labeled with the letters of those false statements (so if you think statement A is false, shade out area A). The remaining lit segments will give you the digital combination required.

Hint: six of the statements are false.

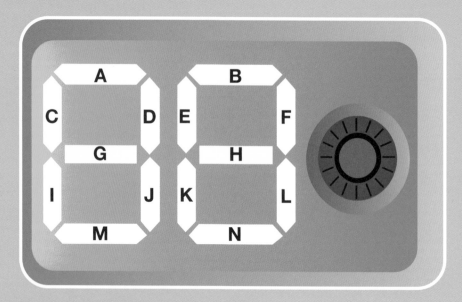

A. The elevator was invented by Otis in 1852.
B. The watt is a unit of power.
C. In heraldry, the color green is referred to as sable.
D. In the Nato phonetic alphabet, Q is for Quebec.
E. The 1988 Olympic Games were held in Los Angeles.
F. Stephane Grapelli was a famous jazz violinist.
G. Rosinante's horse was named Don Quixote.
H. The planet Pluto has one natural satellite called Charon.
I. Tia Maria is a liqueur flavored with oranges.
J. Pathophobia is a fear of diseases.
K. "As old as time itself" is an example of alliteration.
L. St. Boniface is the patron saint of Germany.
M. Coryza is the scientific name for German measles.
N. The United Nations was founded in 1945.

116 DIFFICULTY  7 Minutes

Each block is equal to the sum of the two numbers beneath it. Find all the missing numbers, then figure out the significance of the bottom row.

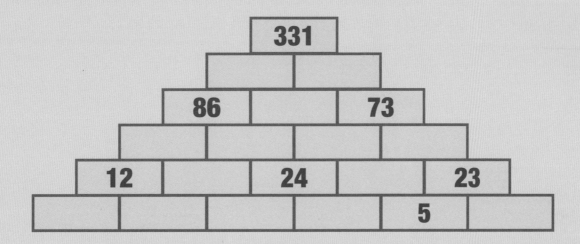

117 DIFFICULTY  3 Minutes

What comes next?

4.5, 1.5, 4.5, 13.5, 10.5, 3.5, 6.5, ?

118 DIFFICULTY ✪✪✪✪✪✪✪✪✪✪  **2** Minutes

Which number is the odd one out?

8567   6589

4369   2189

8162   4328

119 DIFFICULTY ✪✪✪✪✪✪✪✪✪✪  **2** Minutes

What number comes next in the sequence?

100, 99.5,

98, 93.5, ?

120 DIFFICULTY ✪✪✪✪✪✪✩✩✩✩  **1** Minute

We've given the cards below different values, so that an ace = 1, a jack = 11, a queen = 12, and a king = 13, while all other cards have the same value as their numbers. Study this arrangement of cards carefully for one minute, then see if you can answer the questions on page 98.

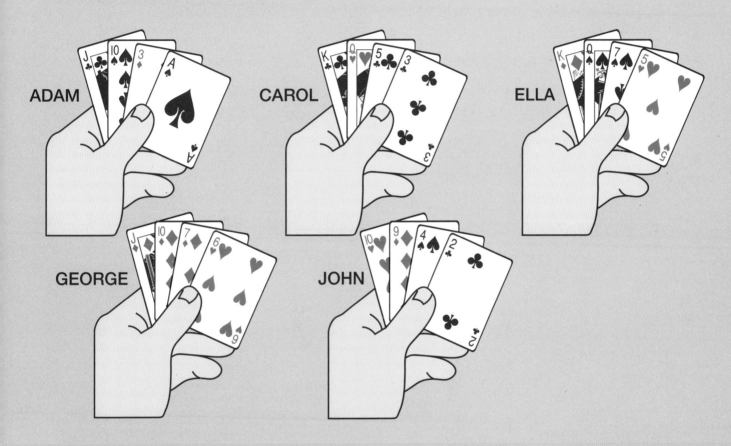

ADAM

CAROL

ELLA

GEORGE

JOHN

121 DIFFICULTY ✪✪✪✪✪✪✪✩✩✪  **5** Minutes

Make a calculation totaling the figure on the right by inserting the four mathematical operators (+, −, ÷, x) between the numbers shown.

They can be inserted in any order, and one of them has been used twice.

| 25 | | 15 | | 87 | | 12 | | 79 | | 44 | = | 147 |

[120] DIFFICULTY ✪✪✪✪✪✪☆☆☆☆  1 Minute

Can you answer these questions about the puzzle on page 97 without looking back?

1. Which player holds the queen of hearts?
2. Only one value of playing card is not represented in any of the five hands. Which one?
3. Which player has cards of the highest total value?
4. Two players hold cards with the same total value: which two players are they, and what is the value of the cards they hold?
5. What is the value of the club in John's hand?
6. Which player holds no black cards?
7. Which player holds the ten of hearts?
8. Only one player has an ace. Which suit is it?

122 DIFFICULTY ✪✪✪✪✪✪✪☆☆☆  3 Minutes

Each block is equal to the sum of the two numbers beneath it. Can you find all the missing numbers?

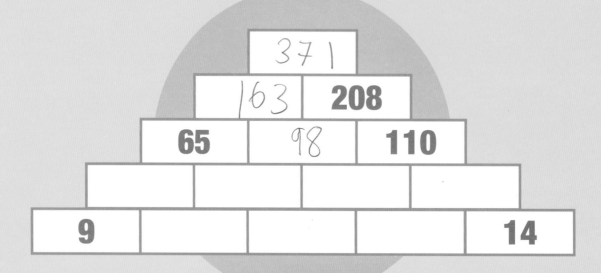

123 DIFFICULTY  5 Minutes

Can you fit these numbers into the grid? One number has already been inserted to help you get started.

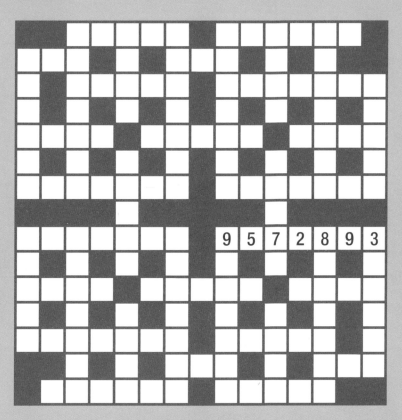

3 DIGITS	5 DIGITS	7 DIGITS
516	16466	1956723
552	24538	2675994
746	29534	3945178
793	31498	4281948
	32179	5346342
4 DIGITS	58558	6585144
1424	59383	6636991
2726	68475	7421445
4649	94741	7811294
6775	96796	8263453
6958		8541779
7523	**6 DIGITS**	~~9572893~~
7957	212589	9625251
8613	353652	9745235
	528888	
	712147	

124 DIFFICULTY ✪✪✪✪✪✪✪☆☆☆  **5** Minutes

Which of the four boxed figures (a, b, c, or d) completes the set?

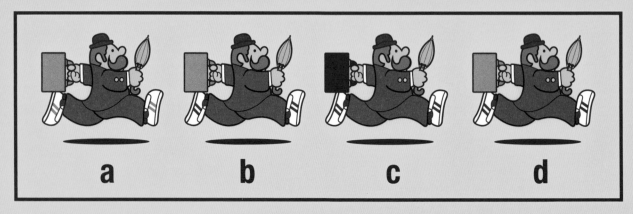

a   b   c   d

125 DIFFICULTY ✪✪✪✪✪✩✩✩✩✩  **8** Minutes

Solve the maze by filling the blank spaces with the four squares below so that the colors run from the top to the bottom in the correct order. The squares below may not be the right way up!

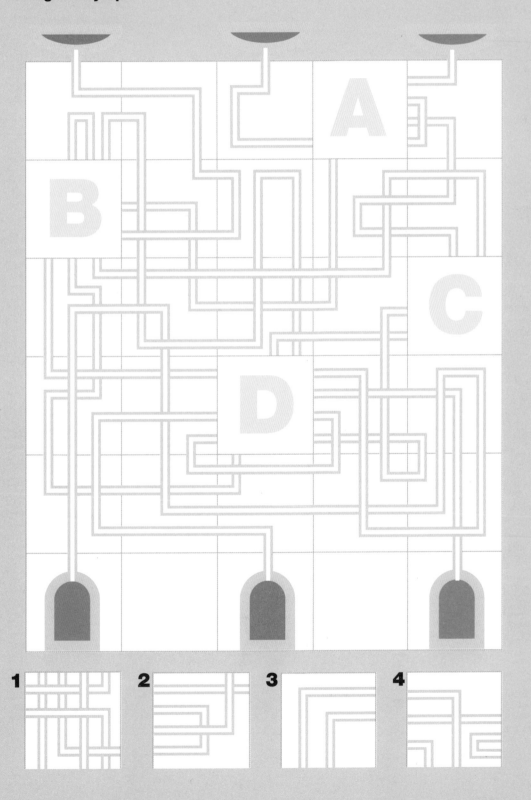

126 DIFFICULTY ✪✪✪✪✪☆☆☆☆☆

Take a number of coins and place them in a circle with a different coin at the top. Two players take turns removing one, two, or three touching coins from the circle. The special coin must be taken last. The player who removes this coin at the very end of the game is the winner.

127 DIFFICULTY ✪✪✪✪✪✪✪✪✪✪

 **1** Minute

One hour ago, it was as long after 1 p.m. as it was before 1 a.m. What time is it now?

128 DIFFICULTY ✪✪✪✪✪✪✪✪✪✪

 **3** Minutes

Which number is the odd one out?

a. 391221

b. 831114

c. 491322

d. 191029

e. 891726

f. 931215

129 DIFFICULTY ✪✪✪✪✪✪✪☆☆☆  **4** Minutes

Place the remaining tiles into the grid given that:
* there is one square of every color in every row and column, and
* each row, column, and main diagonal adds up to 34.

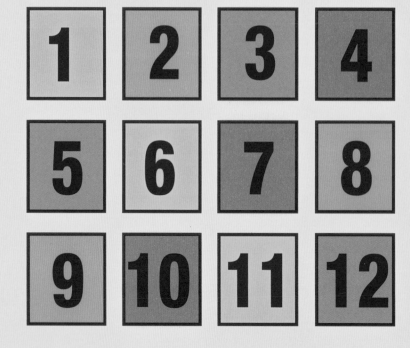

130 DIFFICULTY ✪✪✪✪✪✪✪✪✪✪  **5** Minutes

Write the numbers from 1 to 10 onto the bricks so that each block in the upper three rows contains the (positive) difference between the two numbers beneath it.

For example, if the top block was a 5, the blocks in the second row could be 7 and 2.

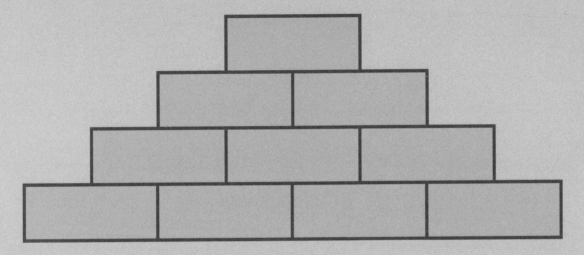

131 DIFFICULTY ✪✪✪✪✪✪✪✪✪✪  **3** Minutes

7296384 is to 3987462

as 6174258 is to 2756841

and 2917834 is to ?

ANSWERS

1

Square A is the correct move. It forces a win for Os. The other options will force a draw or possibly even a loss.

2

The combination is 29. Correct versions of false statements:

C. A league equals three nautical miles.

J. Hexadecimal is the number system for counting in groups of 16.

K. An obtuse angle has between 90 and 180 degrees.

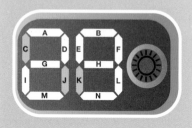

3

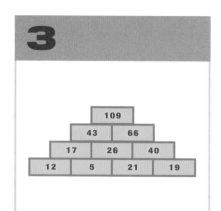

```
            109
         43     66
      17    26    40
   12    5    21    19
```

4

a; the dots change places in pairs working clockwise and starting with the top left/top middle dots.

5

| | 6 | 1 | 6 | 0 | 5 | | 8 | 9 | 7 | 0 | 3 | 0 |
|1|3|5| |1| |2|0|8| |9| |2| |
|3| |8|2|3|1|4| |2|6|7|8|3|7|4|
|0| |3| |4| |4| |2| |9| |5| |3|
|4|2|2|5| |3|2|7|9|1| |9|4|8|4|
|7| |2| |2| |4| |9| |2| |8| |2|
1	7	6	7	4	6	3		7	2	1	6	8	6	0
				4					2					
9	7	2	1	3	0	5		4	9	6	5	9	0	7
0		0		7		9		9		6		1		6
5	8	9	0		7	9	9	3	7		2	2	4	6
5		6		1		7		7		8		4		8
6	7	9	6	5	8	8		5	5	1	5	9		6
		1		4		4	2	4		9		6	5	0
	5	3	0	3	9	5		1	8	9	1	5	

6

7

8

Flo's animal is a chicken. The chicken was 2nd, so Flo was also 2nd (clue 1). Spot is a pig. Spot the pig didn't come 5th or 1st (2). Jack has a calf, and it placed 5th, so Jack placed 5th (3). Bob's animal is named Guffy, and it placed 4th, so Bob placed 4th (3). Norbert is a sheep, and his owner isn't Mavis or Flo (4), Guffy isn't a pig (2) or a sheep (4), and Bob doesn't have a calf (3) or a chicken (1). So Guffy must be a goat. Mavis doesn't own the chicken (1), the calf (3), or the sheep (4), and Bob owns the goat, so Mavis must own the pig, leaving Ned with Norbert the sheep. Mavis and Spot didn't come 5th or 1st (2), or 2nd (1), or 4th (3), so they came 3rd, leaving Ned and Norbert the sheep 1st. Guffy was 4th (3), and Tizzy placed higher than Pong (5), so Tizzy was 2nd and a chicken (1) and Pong was 5th and a calf (3).

Norbert—sheep—1st—Ned
Tizzy—chicken—2nd—Flo
Spot—pig—3rd—Mavis
Guffy—goat—4th—Bob
Pong—calf—5th—Jack

9

1. 4
2. 4+15+19=38
3. 4x19=76
4. Triangle (4) and cross (38)
5. 72
6. 7
7. The orange triangle and the orange cross
8. 89

10

Ten past one. Between any two clocks, 25, then 35, 45, 55, etc. minutes are added.

11

Nobel Peace Prize

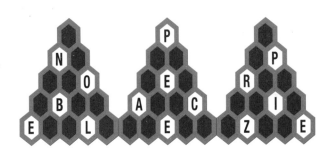

12

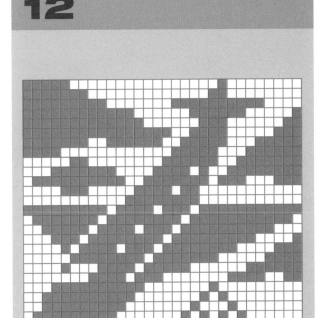

13

c; the figure retains the same shape, however, small circles change to large circles and vice versa.

14

They start and end with the same letter:

9:57   Nine fifty-seveN
8:23   Eight twenty-threE
1:32   One thirty-twO
11:25   Eleven twenty-fivE
9:13   Nine thirteeN
2:48   Two forty-eighT

15

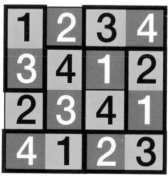

16

d; each vertical and horizontal line contains two dark-skinned and one light-skinned face.

Each line contains a face with one freckle, a face with two freckles, and a face with three freckles. Each line contains two eyes with two round highlights and one with a single round highlight. Finally, each line contains a blue eye, a brown eye, and a green eye. The missing image should be dark skinned with one freckle and a blue eye with two round highlights.

17

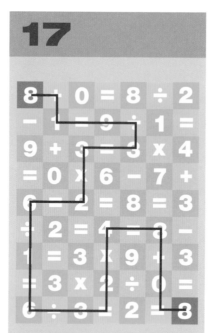

18

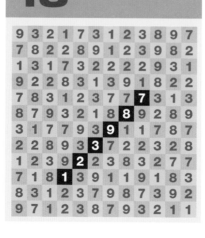

19

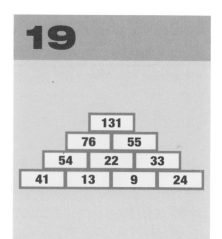

20

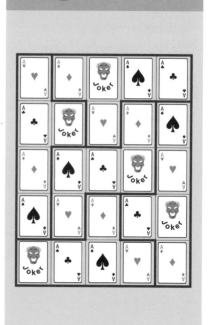

21

| 9 | − | 3 | + | 6 | ÷ | 2 | − | 4 | x | 5 | = | 10 |

22

10; one square and one circle weigh as much as five triangles. Thus one square weighs as much as three triangles, so a circle weighs as much as two triangles. Therefore, ten circles are needed to balance scale c.

23

d; a is the same string of dots as e, and b is the same string as c.

24

b; each vertical and horizontal line contains one red spade and two black ones. Each line also contains one image where the heart and club have been reversed and one image where the diamond has been turned on its side. The missing image should have a red spade, the club and heart should be reversed, and the diamond should be the right way up.

25

	1	3	1	5	2			4	4	2	2	8	2	
6	9	3		9		2	2	6		4		2		
1		6	0	9	8	3		5	8	7	1	1	6	4
6		5		3		9		3		6		8		2
9	3	7	9		2	7	8	5	6		4	3	6	8
3		0		5		5		0		1		6		4
7	6	3	8	6	6	3		4	7	2	0	9	5	2
				9					9					
3	3	6	8	2	8	7		9	4	6	5	2	6	8
5		9		2		7		2		8				8
3	4	6	5		9	1	3	0	9		7	4	5	6
6		0		5		0		2		6		5		0
5	5	2	1	6	6	1		8	9	1	1	6		3
	4		7		1	3	9		0		8	0	9	
3	2	0	7	3	0		7	2	7	7	6			

26

The gold item Dupris wore was not Tom Buick (8), Canale (8), Fundi, or Armande (7), so it must have been Vergucci and a bag (4). The black item was not then Vergucci, or Tom Buick (9), Canale (6), or Armande, so it must have been Fundi. The pink hat wasn't Tom Buick or Fundi (2), Vergucci (4), nor Armande (5), so it must have been Canale. The red item must then have been Armande and Manon's. The pink hat wasn't Jody's (6), Kate's (2), Naomi Taylor's (8), or Manon's (5), so it must have been Emma's and she must be Emma Briant (8). Naomi Taylor wasn't then wearing a hat, gloves, or shoes (3), or the bag (belonging to Dupris)—she must have been wearing the coat. Naomi Taylor's coat must have been blue, as it wasn't pink (2), gold (7), black (6), or red (Manon). So Naomi was also wearing Tom Buick (9) and the gold bag was Kate's, making her Kate Dupris (7). The gloves weren't then blue, pink (2), red (5), gold (bag), or blue (coat), so they must have been black and Fundi

and belong to Jody (6), and the shoes must be red and Armande and belong to Manon. Ms. Jones didn't wear gloves (1), so the red shoes are hers, making her Manon and leaving the Fundi gloves to Ms. Heaton, who must then be Jodie.

Jody Heaton—Fundi—gloves—black
Kate Dupris—Vergucci—bag—gold
Naomi Taylor—Tom Buick—coat—blue
Emma Briant—Fundi—bag—pink
Manon Jones—Armande—shoes—red

27

b; the circle moves one corner clockwise, then two corners, then three corners, etc., at each stage and the line moves one corner only counterclockwise at each stage.

28

To win the game, play first and take two coins. Whatever your opponent does, leave 1, 8, or 9 coins (if you have taken an odd number of coins), or 4, 5, or 12 coins (if you have an even number of coins).

29

8; three cherries and one gooseberry balance one banana, thus four gooseberries plus three cherries weigh as much as eleven cherries, and four gooseberries weigh as much as eight

cherries. So two cherries weigh as much as one gooseberry. This gives the equivalent of two-and-a-half gooseberries in scale a balancing one banana, so five gooseberries weigh as much as two bananas. There are two bananas (equal to five gooseberries) and six cherries (equal to three gooseberries) in scale c. Thus eight gooseberries are needed to balance scale c.

30

107; add the digits of the previous number each time, i.e., 49 (+ 4 + 9) = 62, 62 (+ 6 + 2) = 70, 70 (+ 7 + 0) = 77, etc. Therefore 103 (+ 1 + 0 + 3) = 107.

31

5149; in all the others, add the first and third digits to produce the second and fourth digits, for example, 7141, where 7 + 4 = 11.

32

33

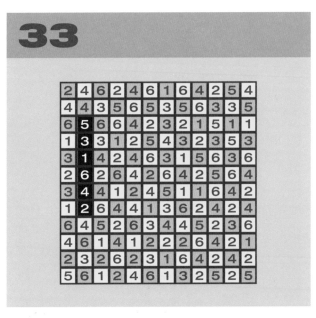

34

35

36

8; one blue ball weighs as much as three yellow balls, so two red balls also weigh as much as three yellow balls, and two red balls weigh as much as one blue ball. Thus eight red balls are needed to balance scale c.

37

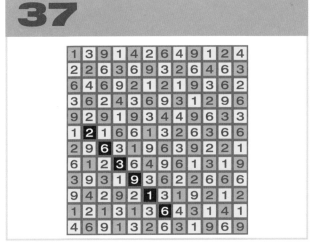

38

39

c; the large 5-sided figure (pentagon) reduces its number of sides by one and becomes a rectangle. The number of dots that are contained in the figure increase by one and change from black to white.

40

43

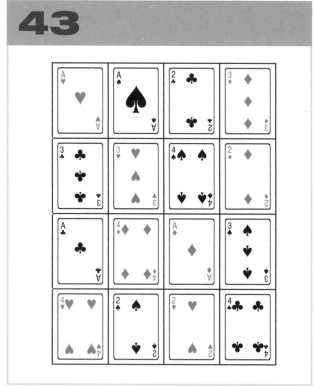

41

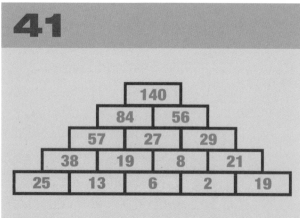

42

The hour hand should point to 7 o'clock. In the series, the minute hand is 30, 60, 90, 120, and 150 degrees clockwise from the hour hand.

44

45

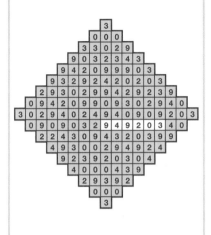

46

e; looking across the line of circles, the top left quarter alternates star/diamond, the top right quarter alternates circle with dot/circle, the bottom left quarter alternates white dot/black dot/dot with line, and the bottom right quarter alternates one line/two lines/three lines horizontally, and three lines/two lines/one line vertically.

47

d; all the others are the same figure rotated.

48

$5000 + 250x = 12000 - 100x$. Hence, $350x = 7000$, so $x = 20$. The numbers will be identical in 20 hours.

49

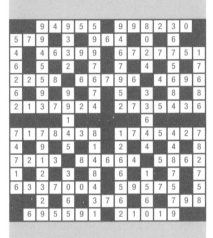

50

The combination is 64. Correct versions of false statements:

B. 39 is not a prime number because it is divisible by 13.

D. 50 divided by 0.5 equals 100.

K. If P x Q = Q, then P must be 1 as long as Q doesn't equal zero.

N. The cube of 5 is 125.

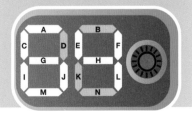

51

Blisterine is Steve's and didn't go 265 mph (1). Zak's last name is Dupris and he didn't go 265 either (1). Van Happs's car is Hot Stuff and it went 240 mph, and Jackson's went 250 mph (2). Marty went 255 mph and Chicken Speed went 235 mph. (3). Neither Blisterine (1), Hot Stuff (2), Chicken Speed (3), nor Fast and Loose (4) went 265 mph, so it must have been Rock Racer. Blisterine didn't go 265, 255, 240, or 235 mph, so it must have gone 250. Schwartz was faster than Delaney (5), so given that neither Dupris (1), Van Happs (2), or Jackson (2) went 265 mph, Schwartz must have. Zak Dupris didn't go 255 mph (3), so he must have gone 235, making his car Chicken Speed and leaving Delaney at 255, making his car Fast and Loose—

and Delaney must be Marty. Both Zak Dupris and Chicken Speed went 235 mph so that must be his car. Blisterine's owner is Steve (1), and Jackson's car and Blisterine both went 250 mph, so Steve is Steve Jackson. Fast and Loose was quicker than Bubba (4), so Bubba must have gone 240 mph, making him Bubba Van Happs, owner of Hot Stuff.

Steve Jackson—250 mph—Blisterine
Zak Dupris—235 mph—Chicken Speed
Bubba Van Happs—240 mph—Hot Stuff
Marty Delaney—255 mph—Fast and Loose
Kate Schwartz—265 mph—Rock Racer.

54

52

53

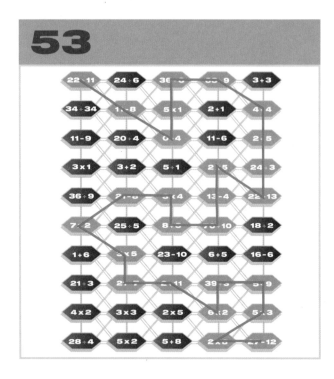

55

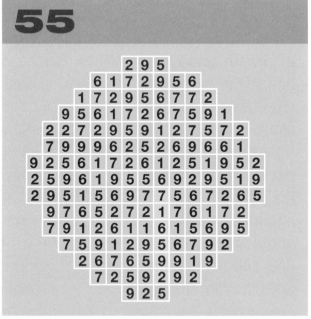

56

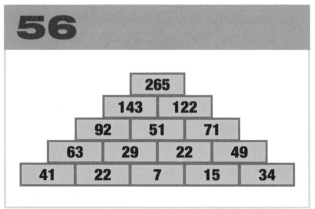

57

Dorrit works in fudge, Brenda doesn't and she isn't Dorrit (1). Diane is Diane Toggle and she doesn't work in wrapping, mints, truffles (2), or fudge (1). Bob works in orders, not with caramels (3). Neither Bob, Brian, nor Brenda work in quality control (4). Deborah, Diane Toggle, and Brenda don't work in lollipops, and Bob and Brian don't work in mints (5). Deborah is Deborah Duffy (6). The taster works in truffles and is not Deborah, Brian, or Bob (6). Bob doesn't work in lollipops (7), caramels (3), mints (5), or truffles (6), so he must work in fudge and fudge must be in orders (3). Neither Deborah Duffy, Diane Toggle, Brenda, nor Bob work in lollipops, so that must be Brian. Button works in packing (8). Caramels are not in wrapping (8). Dorrit isn't Brenda (1), Diane (2), nor Deborah (6), and Brian doesn't work in fudge (1) so Dorrit must be Bob and Dorrit must work in fudge and orders. The truffle worker is neither Diane Toggle (2), Dorrit (1), Deborah Duffy (6), nor Button (8), so it must be Hopper. Hopper then doesn't work with lollipops, and neither do Toggle (5), Duffy (5), nor Bob Dorrit (7), so the lollipop worker must be Button. So Button doesn't work in mints and neither does Bob Dorrit (5), Hopper the truffle taster nor Diane Toggle (2), so Deborah Duffy is the mint worker, leaving Diane Toggle to work in caramels. Diane Toggle doesn't work in wrapping (2), packing (8), or orders (3), and truffles are in tasting so Diane Toggle works in the quality control department, leaving wrapping to Deborah Duffy.

Deborah Duffy—wrapping—mints
Diane Toggle—quality control—caramels
Brenda Hopper—tasting—truffles
Bob Dorrit—orders—fudge
Brian Button—packing—lollipops

58

13; one spade weighs as much as one heart plus one diamond; thus three spades weigh as much as three hearts and three diamonds. So one diamond weighs as much as six hearts and one spade weighs as much as seven hearts. Thus thirteen hearts are needed to balance scale c.

59

9	+	6	x	3	−	7	=	38
−		x		+		x		
3	x	9	+	7	−	6	=	28
x		−		x		−		
6	+	7	−	9	x	3	=	12
+		+		−		+		
7	−	3	x	6	+	9	=	33
=		=		=		=		
43		50		84		48		

60

1. Clubs
2. 2
3. 20: 4, 6, 9, and ace
4. 17: 5, jack, and ace
5. The 6 of hearts
6. 22: queen, 5, 4, and ace
7. Spades
8. The 8 of clubs

61

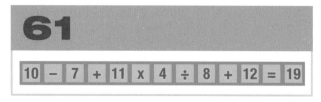

10 − 7 + 11 x 4 ÷ 8 + 12 = 19

62

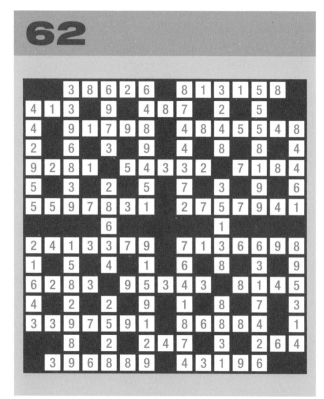

63

d; it contains five empty circles, whereas the other shields only contain four empty circles each.

64

329476; each number is the third, fourth, and fifth digits of the previous number reversed, followed by the first, second, and sixth digits of the previous number in the same order.

65

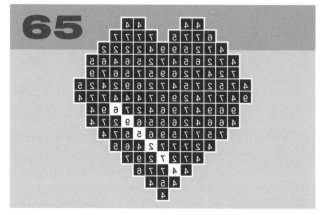

66

The center is very important. Try to restrict the movement of your opponent's coins (e.g., into a corner) so that there's more opportunity to make a winning line.

67

68

20 + 14 − 9 x 6 − 18 ÷ 3 = 44

69

73; they are the digits of the three times table (3, 6, 9, 12, 15, 18, 21, 24, 27, 30) rearranged in groups of two.

70

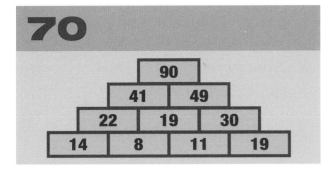

71

Seven minutes past ten. The hour hand points to the number of letters in the city's name. The minute hand points to the value of the first letter (i.e., 1 minute past equals A, 2 minutes past equals B, and so on).

GEORGETOWN

72

b; each vertical line and horizontal line contain two right-side-up pairs of lightning bolts and one inverted pair. Each line contains a black, a white, and a green central oval. Each line contains two green cages and one white wire cage over the oval. Finally, each line contains one image with two buttons, one with a single button, and one with no buttons. The missing image should have a pair of right-side-up lightning bolts and a white central oval with a green cage, and one button.

73

9	2	7
4	6	8
5	10	3

74

	3	9	5	4	4		9	7	9	1	9	8
1	9	7		9		3	1	8		6		6
5		8	2	6	3	2		7	6	7	3	1	8	9
1		5		2		9		3		7		2		7
2	5	9	6		1	2	3	8	2		6	2	4	1
4		4		7		7		9		8		3		8
1	1	2	2	7	5	2		2	2	1	2	9	1	8
				4					7					
5	8	5	3	5	1	1		8	4	5	6	6	1	6
4		8		6		5		1		8		1		6
1	6	3	7		6	3	4	1	6		8	9	1	3
4		8		4		8		4		3		7		2
3	7	9	1	6	6	8		4	9	8	3	3		1
	8		2		8	1	6		2		7	9	5
	2	6	8	2	9	8		2	3	7	4	5	

75

1. Orange
2. 9
3. Pink
4. Blue
5. 8
6. Blue, pink, and orange
7. 7
8. Purple

76

He does his patrols when his digital clock is displaying a palindromic time: 01:10, 02:20, 03:30, 04:40, 05:50, 10:01, 11:11, 12:21.

77

d; every fifth square contains a left diagonal line, every fourth square contains a red dot, and every third square contains a right diagonal line.

78

79

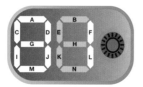

The combination is 81. Correct versions of false statements:

B. IQ stands for Intelligence Quotient.

E. The first Boeing 747 jumbo jet flew in February 1969.

H. A lepidopterist collects butterflies.

K. Omega is the final letter of the Greek alphabet.

N. *Cygnus cygnus* is the Latin classification for the swan.

80

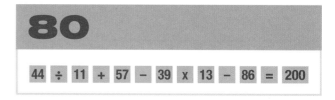

81

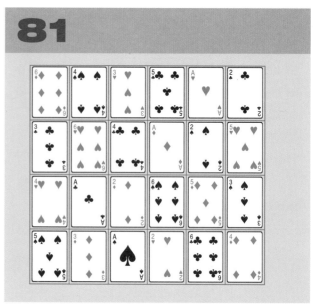

82

9263; all the others follow the pattern:
7421/2471
3869/6839

4283/8243 in which the first and third digits have swapped places.

83

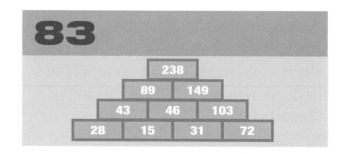

84

9731862; the numbers are rearranged so that all the odd numbers (in numerically descending order) are followed by all the even numbers (in numerically descending order).

85

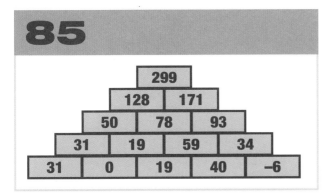

86

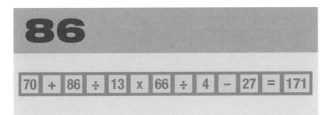

87

Wayne's second name is Brady. He isn't a center forward or a midfielder and he didn't score 1 goal (1). Darius didn't score 5 goals (1). Charlton plays for Rovers; he didn't score 1 goal, and Brady didn't score 5 (2). The center forward plays for Rangers and didn't score 5 or 4 goals (3). The Rovers' player, Charlton, didn't score 1 or 2 (3). Paul plays for United and didn't score 1 goal (4). Hughes scored 4 and isn't a winger (5). The left winger is Emile. He didn't score 1, 2, 5 (6), or 4 goals (5), so he must have scored 3. Callan didn't score 5 (7). Wayne Brady didn't score 1 (1), 5 (2), or 4 (5) goals. Emile scored 3, so Wayne must have scored 2. The Rangers' center forward didn't score 5, 4 (3), 3 (left winger), or 2 (Wayne Brady, not a center forward), so he scored 1. Paul scored one more than David, neither scored 2 (Wayne) or 3 (Emile) goals, so Paul must have scored 5 for United and David 4, leaving Darius with 1, which makes him the Rangers' center forward. The Rovers player scored two more than Darius (3), giving him 3 and making him Emile, in which case the Town player scored 4 (6). This leaves the City defender (7) with 2, making him Wayne Brady. Hughes scored 4 (5), so he's the Town player named David. Callan got 1 (7), making him Darius, the Rangers' center forward. Best then plays for United, making him Paul with 5 goals, and since neither Callan (center forward), Brady (defender), Hughes (5), nor Charlton (left wing) are right wingers, Paul Best must be one and David Hughes must be the midfielder for Town.

Wayne Brady—City—defender—2 goals
David Hughes—Town—midfield—4 goals
Paul Best—United—right wing—5 goals
Darius Callan—Rangers—center forward—1 goal
Emile Charlton—Rovers—left wing—3 goals

88

14	x	5	+	33	−	19	÷	4	+	15	=	36

89

3527; in all of the others, the sum of the first two digits is equal to the sum of the second two digits, e.g., 3984, where 3 + 9 = 8 + 4.

90

8; one knife and one fork weigh as much as six spoons, so two knives and one fork weigh as much as five forks. Thus one knife weighs as much as two forks. Three forks thus balance six spoons and one fork balances two spoons. Thus eight spoons are needed to balance scale c.

91

92

To decode, you type the message on the keyboard but move your fingers one key to the left each time. For example, a W becomes a Q instead. The deciphered message reads as follows: "The code word is a city in New York state, which is described as a bison in the US." Therefore, the code word is BUFFALO.

93

6947; reverse the digits and discard the smallest value digit each time.

94

95

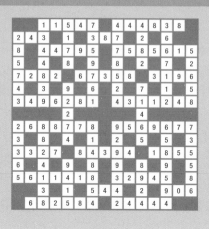

96

1217; 5 + 7 = 12; 9 + 8 = 17

97

Cards that have moved are shown shaded.

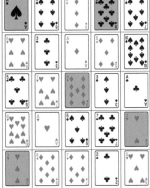

98

Bobby is Bobby Macfie and he played marbles. Bobby Macfie wasn't 4th or 5th and he and the marbles were not on the soccer field (1). The 3rd place finisher was in the common room, and it wasn't Wendy nor Betsy (2). The 4th place was hopscotch, not Wendy nor Betsy nor with the last name Stuart (3). The Hacky Sack player was not named Stuart and not 5th, and jump rope wasn't 1st (4). Wendy was in the playground. She isn't Macdonald or Macfie (5). Betsy is Betsy Campbell, wasn't 1st, didn't play hopscotch, and wasn't in the cafeteria (6). Billy was 1st, but not in Hacky Sack, marbles, nor on the soccer field (7). Billy wasn't 4th, and neither was Bobby (1), Wendy, nor Betsy (3), so it must have been William and he must have been playing hopscotch (3).

Jump rope was in the quad and not done by William, Billy, or Bobby (8). Hacky Sack wasn't Billy, Betsy, or Bobby, or played in the cafeteria or common room (9). Hacky Sack, marbles (7), jump rope (4), and hopscotch (3) weren't 1st, so jacks must have been, and jacks must be Billy (7). Betsy wasn't then jacks nor hopscotch (6), marbles (1), nor Hacky Sack (9), so she must have been jumping rope in the quad (8). Wendy wasn't skipping then, and she wasn't playing hopscotch (3), marbles (1), or jacks (Billy), so she must be Hacky Sack. Hacky Sack finished higher than jump rope (4), neither were 1st (7 & 4) or 4th (3), jump rope wasn't 3rd (2), and so Hacky Sack was 2nd and jump rope was 5th (Betsy Campbell in the quad), leaving marbles with 3rd—in the common room (2) with Bobby Macfie (1). Stuart isn't marbles (1), Hacky Sack (4), hopscotch (3), nor jump rope (Betsy Campbell), so must be jacks and thus 1st and Billy. Wendy isn't Macfie (1), Campbell (6), Macdonald, nor Macfie, so she must be Lewis and William must be Macdonald. So:
Bobby Macfie—3rd—common room—marbles
Billy Stuart—1st—cafeteria—jacks
Wendy Lewis—2nd—playground—Hacky Sack
Betsy Campbell—5th—quad—jump rope
William Macdonald—4th—soccer field—hopscotch.

99

100

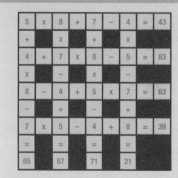

101

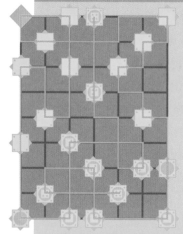

The solution path starts and finishes with the full design: first visiting designs that have had one element removed until just a background shape remains, then replacing the elements until the design is once more complete.

102

When choosing a word, remember that words with a small number of vowels will be more difficult to guess. Examples of five-letter words with no vowels include DRYLY, HYMNS, NYMPH, and TRYST. Do not change your guesses too radically otherwise you will find it difficult to figure out the logic. If you can, move one letter and change another letter completely.

103

d; each vertical and horizontal line contains two white pigs and a pink one. Each line contains two pink-nosed pigs and a white-nosed pig. Each line contains a pig with black feet, a pig with white feet, and a pig with pink feet. Each line contains two pigs with four spots and one with three spots. Each line has two pigs facing left and one facing right. Finally, each line contains two pigs with a tail and one with no tail. The missing pig should be white, with a white nose, white feet, four spots, be facing left, and have a tail.

104

2634 and 16; the two-figure numbers in the top group are the sum of the digits of each of the four-figure numbers in the bottom group and vice versa. For example, 7529/23 (7 + 5 + 2 + 9 = 23).

105

M minutes per mile = (60/M) mph = (60 x 1.6/M) km/h = M km/h. This simplifies to M being the square root of 96 (approx. 9.8). In other words, around 9.8 minutes per mile is the same rate as 9.8 km/h.

106

			119			
		53		66		
	24		29		37	
11.5		12.5		16.5		20.5
3	8.5	4	12.5	8		

107

17
05
Looking across at numbers in the same position in each block, the series of numbers progress: 7, 5, 3, 1, (−2); 4, 5, 6, 7 (+1); 9, 6, 3, 0 (−3); 8, 7, 6, 5 (−1).

108

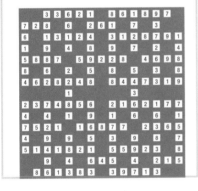

109

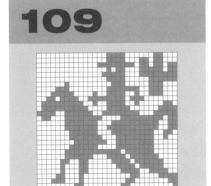

110

1	8	15	10
11	14	5	4
6	3	12	13
16	9	2	7

111

13	+	12	x	25	−	16	=	609
+		x				+		
25	−	16	x	12	+	13	=	121
−		+			+	x		
12	x	13	+	16	−	25	=	147
x		−		x		−		
16	+	25	−	13	x	12	=	336
=		=		=		=		
416		180		377		713		

112

92 and 81; in all the others the number at the bottom is produced by taking the second digit of the top number less 1, followed by the first digit of the top number less 1.

113

Strangely, the only possible solution turns out to be 2:12. This works because the hour hand moves one "tick" clockwise after every 12 minutes. At 2 o'clock, the hour hand is ten ticks around the clock. At 2:12, it will be 11 ticks around, and the minute hand will be at the 12th tick. Therefore, the hands are exactly one tick apart.

114

c; rotate the grid 90 degrees clockwise, then deduct 1 from the odd numbers and add 1 to the even numbers.

115

The combination is 73.
Correct versions of false statements:
C. In heraldry, the color green is referred to as vert.
E. The 1984 Olympic Games were held in Los Angeles.
G. Don Quixote's horse was named Rosinante.
I. Tia Maria is a liqueur flavored with coffee.

K. "As old as time itself" is an example of a simile.

M. Coryza is the scientific name for the common cold.

116

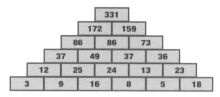

Decipher the bottom row using the system A = 1, B = 2, C = 3, etc., which spells out the word CIPHER.

117

19.5; the sequence progresses: divide by 3/add 3/multiply by 3/subtract 3.

118

6589; in all the others the number formed by the middle two digits is the product (multiplied together) of the first and last digits, for example, 8567, where 8 x 7 = 56.

119

80; subtract 0.5, then 1.5, then 4.5, then 13.5, i.e., the amount subtracted is multiplied by 3 each time.

120

1. Carol
2. An 8
3. Ella (card values total 37)
4. Adam and John (card values total 25)
5. 2
6. George
7. John
8. Spades

121

25 x 15 − 87 ÷ 12 + 79 + 44 = 147

122

The top three levels are straightforward. For the other numbers we need to employ a different approach. One method is to replace the three unknowns with the letters A, B, and C. This gives us these three equations:
$65 = (9 + A) + (A + B)$, hence $2A + B = 56$;
$98 = (A + B) + (B + C)$, hence $A + 2B + C = 98$;
$110 = (B + C) + (C + 14)$, hence $B + 2C = 96$.
Adding the first and last equation together gives $2A + 2B + 2C = 152$, hence $A + B + C = 76$.

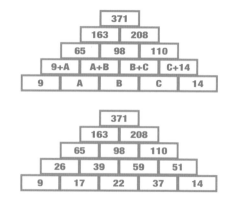

Comparing this with the middle equation shows that B must be 22, since it has another B and its total is 22 higher. Now that we know B = 22, it's easy to see that A = 17 and C = 37 from the other equations. The rest of the pyramid can now be completed.

123

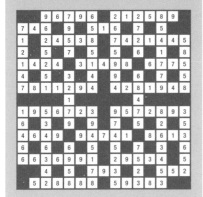

124

d; each vertical and horizontal line contains a green, a blue, and a red umbrella. Each line contains a brown, a black, and a gray briefcase. Each line contains two black hats and a blue one. Each line contains two pairs of sneakers with dark blue stripes and one pair with red stripes. Each line contains one image with missing cuff buttons. Finally, each line has one of the three images facing right. The missing image should have a green umbrella, a gray suitcase, a black hat, blue striped sneakers, and cuff buttons and should be facing right.

125

Square 1 goes in position D, 2 to A, 3 to C, and 4 to B.

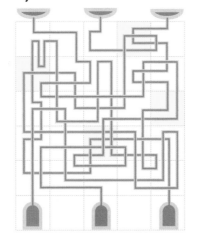

126

With an odd number of coins, making moves that are the mirror-image to your opponent's will guarantee a win.

127

8 p.m.; since this is one hour later than the midpoint between 1 p.m and 1 a.m., namely 7 p.m.

128

d, 191029; in all the others, add the first two numbers to produce the number formed by the third and fourth digits, then add again to produce the number formed by the fifth and sixth digits. For example 3 + 9 = 12, and 9 +12 = 21, this producing the number 391221.
Option d, following this rule, should be 191019, not 191029.

129

130

Here is one possible solution:

		3			
	7		4		
	2		9		5
8		10		1		6

131

8132479; the positions of the numbers move as follows:

A	B	C	D	E	F	G
7	2	9	6	3	8	4
6	1	7	4	2	5	8
2	9	1	7	8	3	4

E	C	F	A	G	D	B
3	9	8	7	4	6	2
2	7	5	6	8	4	1
8	1	3	2	4	7	9

ACKNOWLEDGMENTS ✪ CONFOUNDING LOGIC

✪ Puzzle contributors

Contributors are listed next to the numbers of the puzzles they created.

✪ David Bodycombe

Puzzles 1, 2, 3, 10, 11, 14, 15, 19, 28, 38, 41, 42, 48, 50, 56, 66, 70, 71, 73, 76, 78, 79, 83, 85, 91, 92, 102, 105, 106, 110, 113, 115, 116, 122, 126, 127, 129, 130

✪ Guy Campbell

Puzzles 8, 12, 16, 17, 24, 26, 40, 44, 51, 53, 54, 57, 67, 72, 87, 98, 101, 103, 109, 124, 125

✪ Philip Carter

Puzzles 4, 13, 23, 27, 30, 31, 39, 46, 47, 63, 64, 69, 77, 82, 84, 89, 93, 96, 104, 107, 112, 114, 117, 118, 119, 128, 131

✪ Probyn Puzzles

Puzzles 5, 6, 7, 21, 25, 32, 34, 35, 49, 52, 59, 61, 62, 68, 74, 80, 86, 88, 95, 99, 100, 108, 111, 121, 123

✪ Puzzler Media Ltd

Puzzles 9, 18, 20, 22, 29, 33, 36, 37, 43, 45, 55, 58, 60, 65, 75, 81, 90, 94, 97, 120

Confounding Logic was commissioned, edited, designed, and produced by:
Book Creation Ltd., 20 Lochaline Street, London W6 9SH, United Kingdom

Managing Director: Hal Robinson

Editor: David Popey **Art Editor:** Keith Miller

Designer: Justin Hunt **Copy Editor:** Sarah Barlow **Editorial Assistants:** Claire Bratt, Rosemary Browne